ry
of the
Falklands

Illustrated with the stamps depicting that aspect of history, together with maps and photographs

by

G. D. Moir DFC, FRGS, FRPSL.

Printed by
ChrisPrint, Croydon
1995

First edition published 1993 by
G. D. Moir
Croydon, Surrey.

2nd edition 1995

British Library Cataloguing Data.
A catalogue record for this book is available from the British Library

ISBN 0 9521554 0 0

Typeset by J.E.Davey
in Times using an Olivetti PCS33 computer
and Aldus Pagemaker v4.0 software.

Geoffrey Moir

Geoffrey Moir was born in Croydon in 1921, being educated at The Croydon Boys' High School. First enjoying employment with the Croydon Gas Co., upon the outbreak of World War II, he volunteered for service with the Royal Air Force, serving as a member of a Lancaster Pathfinder aircraft in which he completed no fewer than 60 missions, being awarded the D.F.C. and Bar.

Returning to civilian life, he entered the teaching profession, spending the first few years at Woodside Primary School before transferring to Ashburton High School becoming a Senior Master teaching English, finally retiring in 1982.

His life-long hobby and interests have been travel and philately. Specialising in the postage stamps and postal history of the Falkland Islands, the Dependencies and British Antarctic Territory, he was determined to visit those Islands when he retired. Initially the Conflict prevented that, until being asked to re-open a school on remote West Falkland for a period of six months. He became so fascinated with the Islands, their way of life and its prodigious wildlife that he remained for four years, only then returning through a deterioration of health.

Since his return to the United Kingdom he has devoted his life to furthering knowledge of the Islands to others all over the country. He gained his Fellowship of the Royal Geographic Society in 1975, and Fellowship of the Royal Philatelic Society of London two years later.

Foreword

Sir Rex Hunt C.M.G.
Governor of the Falkland Islands, 1980 - 1985

I first met Geoff Moir in the Falkland Islands after the 1982 conflict. He was one of a gallant band of volunteers who came out in the aftermath of war to help us to get back to normal. He took a teaching post in Fox Bay, where he fell seriously ill and had to be flown into Stanley. The hospital had been razed to the ground by a mad military arsonist and we had rigged up a temporary ward in the Town Hall. I visited him there and was immediately struck by his courage and good cheer. Nothing could dampen his enthusiasm for the place or the people.

It is no exaggeration to say that he fell in love with the Falkland Islands. As readers will see from this little booklet, the love affair continues.

I thought I knew a lot about the Islands, but I was amazed at the variety of titbits contained herein that I had neither read nor heard about before. I did not know, for example, that a German line had carried the Royal Mail to and from the colony for twenty years, or that the male Sperm Whale was twice the size of the female while, with the Blue Whale, it was the other way round.

I had not realised that, in the early days of the First World War, the then Governor had decreed that all public houses would be closed 'for the further efficiency of the Defence Force'. I would have lost all my friends if I had done that in 1982!

There is something for everybody in this book. Geoff obviously found it a labour of love to write and it gives me pleasure to start it off with this Foreword.

Falkland Islands History Through Philately

by G. Moir D.F.C., F.R.G.S., F.R.P.S.L.

The Falkland Islands lie in the South Atlantic between 51 degrees South and 53 degrees South, (and it may be noticed that the latitude of London is 51.5 degrees North). They are about 300 miles east and somewhat to the north of the Straits of Magellan, and a similar distance from the nearest point on the South American mainland. There are two main Islands --- East and West Falkland --- which are divided by the Falkland Sound, and about 200 smaller Islands and islets. The area is approximately 4,700 square miles, about that of Northern Ireland or approximately two-thirds of Wales.

The Islands have a deeply indented coast and possess many harbours and anchorages. The surface is hilly, attaining its maximum elevation of 2,312 ft. in Mt. Usborne on East Falkland. There are no navigable rivers. The entire country is covered with wild moorland interrupted with outcrops of rocks and the peculiar collections of angular boulders called 'stone runs'. Outside Stanley, where practically every house has a garden, there is no cultivation except in the immediate vicinity of the farm settlements and shepherds' houses, where vegetables and, in some places, oats and grass for hay are grown. The soil is chiefly peat. In general appearance the Islands are rather bare, but nevertheless can look attractive whilst the scenery is similar to that of the Shetland Islands. The only town is Stanley, the capital, situated on a harbour entered from Port William on the east side of the group. Smaller settlements have been established throughout the Colony as the headquarters of the various farm settlements; of these the largest is Goose Green, with a population of about 100.

S.H. 105; S.G.175.

The average temperature, 43°F, is low because it does not, on the whole, become as hot in summer as it does in England. The difference in climate between winter and summer is not so pronounced. Temperatures below 20°F are uncommon, even in mid-winter, because of the maritime exposure, and for the same reason summer maxima rarely exceeds 70°F. The average wind speed, day and night, throughout the year in Stanley, exceeds 15 knots, and wind reaches force 6 about two thirds of the days in the year, though severe gales are less common than in some exposed coastal districts of the U.K. Precipitation is seldom heavy and is fairly evenly spread throughout the year, but spring and summer seasons are noted for settled spells of dry sunny weather with fresh winds. The average rainfall, less than London, is about 25 inches. The sun shines on average for 1,650 hours during a year, whereas in England the average is only 1,484, the atmosphere being remarkably clear.

The population is almost wholly British in origin, and totals approximately 2,200 people.

About half of them live in Stanley; the remainder are divided between East and West Falklands and their respective Islands. The Islands are linked by daily air services and coastal shipping, and on East Falkland a road network is developing. There are regular direct air services to Britain and Chile.

The land is used for sheep farming and the production of wool of very high quality. The largest source of income at present, however, is derived from the licensing and control of fishing within a fishery conservation zone. Exploration for offshore oil commenced in 1993 and may well in the next decade become an important resource.

The unique Falkland Islands wildlife --- penguins, seals and seabirds --- is protected and greatly valued by the Islanders, and is the basis of a summer tourist industry. The Islands are visited by cruise ships and by tourists mainly coming by air from Britain. There are simple hotels in Stanley and tourist lodges in the country, some of which offer outstanding sea trout fishing. The scenery is very much that of the Highlands of Scotland.

Stanley itself, with twelve hundred inhabitants, is a busy little town sometimes described as the only English village in the Southern Hemisphere. Stanley is linked by road to Mount Pleasant Airport, which is also the base for the military garrison.

S.H. 440; S.G. 503.

The new school, opened in Heritage Year, 1992, and which includes the public swimming pool and public library, was paid for out of the Islands' fishery revenues. Any British town would be proud of a building of this quality. The Director of Education is a Falkland Islander and the dedicated staff include teachers from other Commonwealth countries as well as Britain.

The Islanders are investing in their future and giving the highest priority to the education of their children.

FIRST SIGHTING AND DISCOVERY

The first recorded evidence of discovery of the Falkland Islands, and therefore that generally accepted, is that by the Elizabethan navigator, John Davis, second in command of the "DESIRE", on 14 August, 1592. He was making his way from Port Desire to the Straits of Magellan when John Jayne, his chronicler, records: "on the 9th we had a sore storm so that we were constrained to hull for our sailes were not to indure any force. The 14th we were driven in among certaine islands never before discovered by any known relation, lying fifty leagues or better from the shore east and northerly from the straits, in which place unless it had pleased God of His wonderful mercie to have ceased the winds, we must of necessity have perished."

S.G. 664.

The legend on the Falkland Islands flag and Coat-of-Arms "Desire the Right" and the ship which appears as part of the Arms refers to this discovery and to "DESIRE". The "DESIRE" was part of the fleet commanded by Cavendish who held the commission of Queen Elizabeth I to attack the Spanish possessions in the Pacific.

Captain John Davis was an explorer and navigator of note, after whom Davis Strait in the Canadian Arctic is named. The Falkland Islands became widely known as 'Davis Southern Land' and it was quite probably from this report or that of Sir Richard Hawkins two years later that the Spaniards first learned of the existence of the Falkland Islands.

S.G. 662.

Sir Richard Hawkins in "DAINTY" followed up John Davis's discovery in 1594, making a landfall at the Jason Islands, sailing past Sedge Island and continuing for a day and a night westwards along the northern part of the Islands to the northern entrance of the Falkland Sound which separates West Falkland from East Falkland. He saw and described the striking white rock known as Eddystone Rock off Cape Dolphin "which at first he thought to be a ship under all her sayles." He named it 'White Conduit on Conditehead'. He thought the land was inhabited because he saw several fires ashore. Tussock grass, unfortunately, is frequently set on fire by lightning strikes; and once lit, peaty ground may burn for many years. Hawkins named the land 'Hawkins Maiden-land' in honour of his Queen "in perpetual memory of her chastity and my endevours."

Four years later a Dutch captain, Sebauld de Weert, in the "HET GHELOOVE", which was the only vessel to survive of the famous Dutch 'squadron of five ships' which made a disastrous raid into the Pacific in 1598, also sighted the Jason Islands, naming them the Sebaldines.

The Argentines have put forward an assertion that the discovery of the Falkland Islands must be credited to one of Magellan's captains, Estaban Gomez. The eighteenth century French explorer Antoine de Bougainville expressed the opinion that the first sighting of the Islands could have been made by the Florentine navigator, Amerigo Vespucci; Amerigo Vespucci accompanied a Portuguese expedition in 1501 which, according to his own account, followed the South American coastline to a point 50°S. at the extreme south of Patagonia and then turned back. De Bougainville was basing himself on a later account attributed to Vespucci which is now generally accepted to have been a forgery and, indeed, an invention.

Magellan, who was a Portuguese leading a Spanish expedition in 1519 followed Vespucci's route along the coast and passed through the Straits of Magellan into the Pacific.

S.H. 61; S.G. 131.

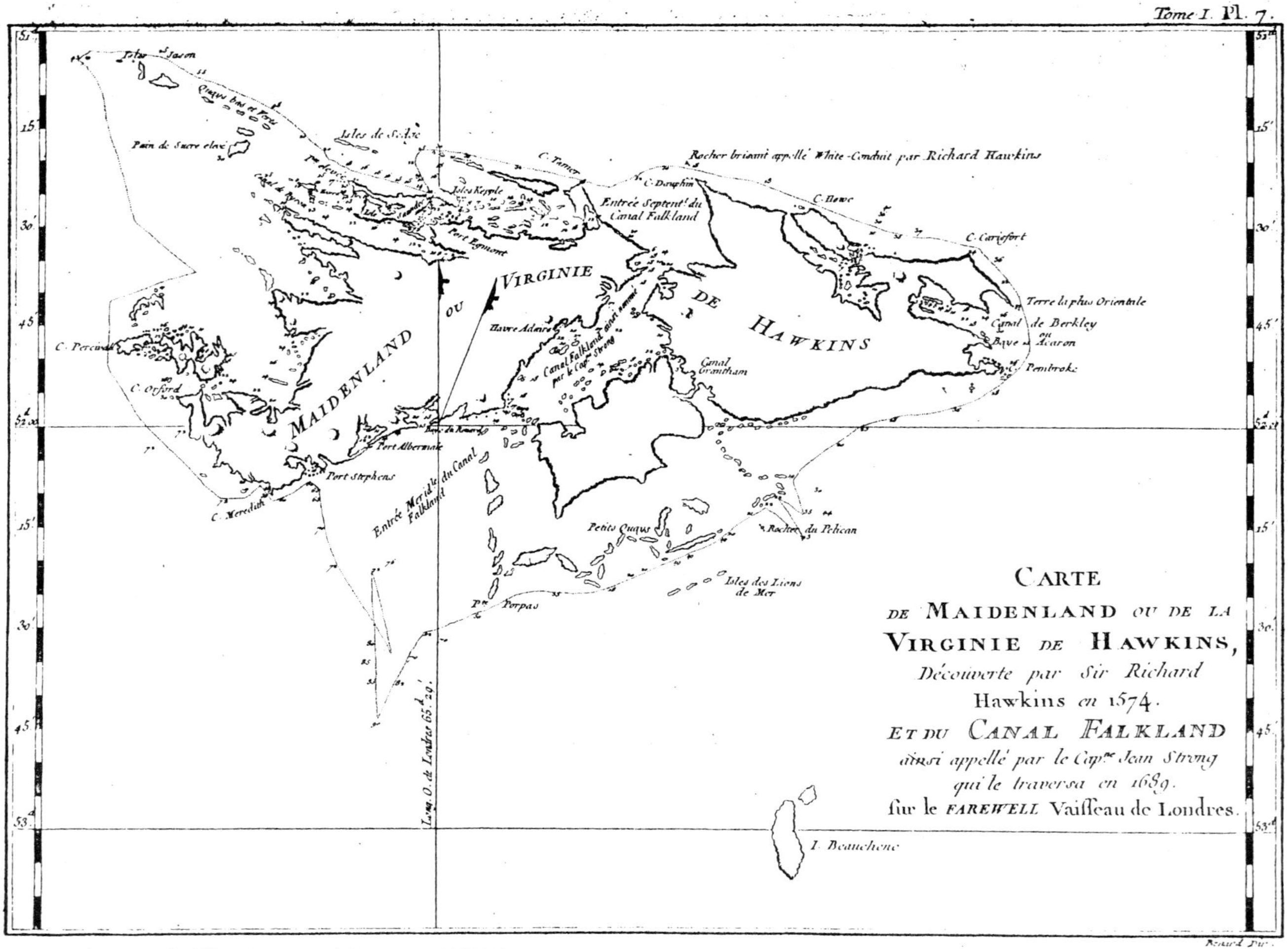

J. Hawkesworth's map (1773) compiled from the voyage of Sir Richard Hawkins.

One of his ships, commanded by Estaban Gomez, turned back and returned to Spain. No more than this is known. Speculation has centred on sixteenth century maps on which an island or islands are marked off the coast of Patagonia and described as Islas se Sanson y Patos or Sanson Islands. The maps are crude even for that time and there is little to indicate suggestion that a description of islands encountered by Camargue's expedition in 1510 could apply to the Falkland Islands.

Sir Francis Drake went round Cape Horn and into the Pacific in 1578, and in 1582 the Spaniards sent a great fleet with 3,500 men and women to establish a garrison in the Straits of Magellan and, as they thought, control access into the Pacific. One of the results of the defeat of the Spanish Armada in 1588 was the abandonment of the garrison. Cavendish in the "DAINTY" found twenty-three of them alive in 1592, the rest having starved to death. Following these disasters the Spaniards abandoned the South Atlantic coast of South America, and left the land to the Indians and the sea to the British, Dutch and French for nearly two centuries, retaining only a hold on the River Plate.

In 1925, the round-the-world yachtsman, Connor O'Brien, using Hawkins's own references, reconstructed his chart, and making adjustments for winds and currents, came to the conclusion it was indeed the Falkland Islands that Hawkins had seen and skirted.

FIRST LANDING, 1690

In 1689, England was unfortunately drawn into the Nine Years War against France, but the Navy was in a state of debt and disrepair. As the war against the enemy's trade was considered as important as military victory, commissions (or letters of Marque) were issued to privateers. One such 'letter of Marque' ordering "General Reprisall's" against the French was issued to Captain John Strong of the sloop "WELFARE", 270-tons and 38 guns. Captain Strong sailed from Plymouth on 1 November, 1689, on a voyage of discovery, making for the Magellan Straits where he hoped to intercept French vessels. On Monday, 27 January, 1690, land was sighted. Captain Strong recorded in his log book that "this land doth show like a great many islands. It is a large land and lyeth East and West nearest, there is severall keys that lye along the shore. We sent our boat on shore to one of them and they brought on board abundance of Pengwind and other fowl and seals..."

The above account is the first recorded landing on what became known as the Falkland Islands, but at the time were known in England as Hawkins Maiden-land. A monument was erected on the spot in 1990, the 300th anniversary. Richard Simson who was on the "WELFARE" also wrote an account of the ship's visit: "As for Hawkins Land, 'tis parted by a great sound which we passed through --- The sound in several places was so full of weeds that the ship could hardly make her way and if one might judge by appearance, there it was we sayled through a meadow..." There were several anxious moments for, as the ship drew three fathoms of water, it grazed the bottom "and the chanel being hard gravel gave us a new but melancholy diversion to the ear, our sayling being for some time extremely rugged and attended with a rattling like that of a hackney carriage on the streets of London."

S.H. 321; S. G. 397.

On Wednesday 29 January,the "WELFARE", which was proceeding down the Sound, 'Fawlkland Sound' as Strong named it in honour of Antony Carey, Fifth Viscount Falkland, Treasurer of the Royal Navy, anchored in a harbour on the west side of the Sound and, according to Strong's log book, "sent out boats on shoar for fresh water and we did kill abundance of Geese and Ducks, but as for wood, there was none. 30th Thursday we rid at anchor at this place filling of fresh water, there is a great many harbours in this Sound..." As far as is known who ever first stepped out of the ship's boat was the first human being to set foot on any part of the Falkland Islands. There is no other earlier record and no one has ever seriously suggested otherwise.

HENRY CARY, LORD FALKLAND.

From an Original Picture by Vansomer

Simson made similar comments about the Islands: "The Island if it were not quite destitute of wood would make a noble plantation: it bears an English name, a good harbour, and a great variety of land and sea fowl." On 1 February, the "WELFARE" cleared the Sound having sailed down its full length and set sail for the Magellan Strait.

In 1701 the French navigator, Jacques Gouinn de Beauchene made the second recorded landed and discovered Beauchene Island, a small island two miles long far to the south east of the main group and the home of enormous numbers of Black Browed Albatross.

Captain Wood Rogers, who sailed around the Falkland Islands in 1708, gave the name Falklands Land to the entire group in his account of his exploration and this became adopted generally, much later being more correctly given as the Falkland Islands.

How the Falkland Islands came to be called 'Islas Malvinas' by the Spanish remains

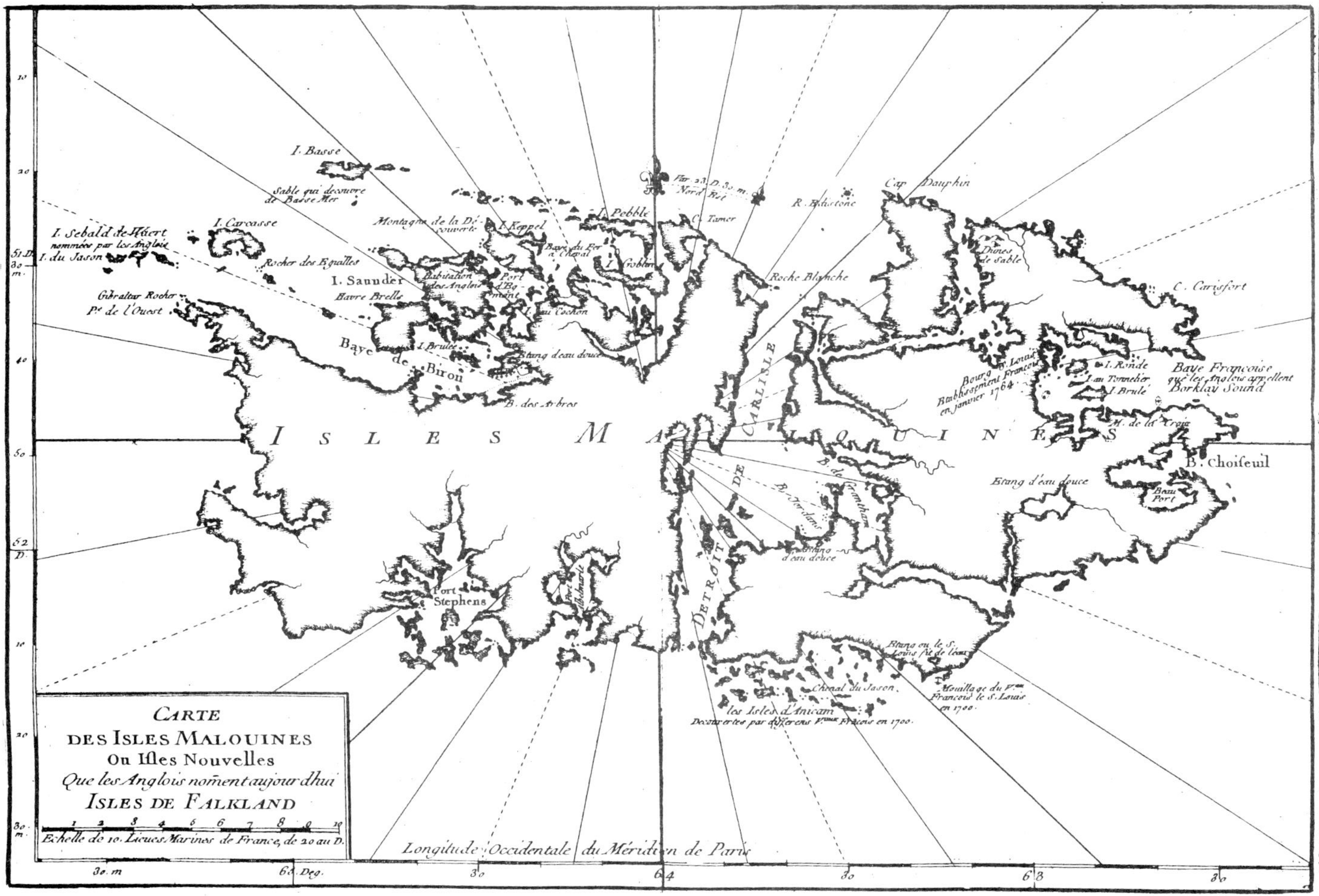

Printed by Bellin (1764) The Petit Atlas Maritime, Paris.

obscure. Islas Malvinas is a hispanisation of 'Iles Malouines', said to be after St. Malo in Brittany. It is not the case that Breton fishermen from St. Malo frequented the Islands in the eighteenth century or any earlier century. The name, if not given to the islands by de Bougainville, seems to have been known to him. The Spanish Government which simply had no name of its own for the Islands, seems simply to have adopted the name he used. In any event the Islands were uninhabited in 1750 and the land was empty --- as it has been since the birth of the world.

S.H.325;S.G.401.

FRENCH AND BRITISH SETTLEMENTS

Lord Anson strongly urged the Admiralty to claim the Falkland Islands in 1740 when he wrote of their possible great importance to shipping; but others were also interested. The young French nobleman, Antoine de Bougainville, deeply resentful of the loss of Quebec, sought, as some degree of compensation, another settlement in those Islands. In 1763, two French ships with 140 crew and settlers from Arcadia in Nova Scotia, and a wide variety of stores, seeds and plants left St. Malo. Stopping at Montevideo, they took on board cattle, pigs, goats and sheep. Land was sighted on 31 January, 1764, and the following day a party set out in search of a suitable settlement site, choosing a small hill at the head of 'Baye Saint-Louis' or Berkeley Sound. In April, following an appropriate ceremony, the fort became known as Port Louis upon Bougainville's departure. By 1767, some 80 persons remained in the settlement. However, under extreme pressure, the French sold Port Louis to the Spaniards in 1766, when its name was changed to Port Soledad (Port Solitary). Traces of the old stone fort are embodied in the present manager's house.

S.H. 314; S.G. 390.

The news of the French settlement reached London shortly after a voyage of exploration had left England comprising the "TAMAR" and "DOLPHIN", sailing on 21 June, 1765. Byron entered the harbour named Port de la Croizade, on Saunders Island, naming it Port Egmont in honour of the First Lord of the Admiralty. At the end of January, Byron continued along the coast naming Cape Tamar, the Eddystone Rock and Cape Dolphin until he, too, came to the entrance to Berkeley Sound. Had he entered he would no doubt have discovered Port Louis, but having coasted the Island and seen no evidence of anyone there he claimed sovereignty of the Islands for Great Britain in the name of King George III.

S.H. 448; S.G. 511.

Spain's reactions were immediate. They demanded the evacuation of both British and French settlements from lands belonging to their Crown by right of Papal Bulls of 1493 and 1506, which had divided the Western Hemisphere between Spain and Portugal; and, in the case of France, Article 6 of their Pacto de Familia. The British however, stood upon their Right

The Tamer and Dolphin at Anchor in Port Egmont.

of Discovery and refused to abandon West Falkland; indeed the Admiralty decided that the occupation of the Falkland Islands was 'the key' to the whole Pacific Ocean.

In the same year, 1765, a further British Expedition was sent to enforce, if necessary, our rights of sovereignty by virtue of discovery, under the command of Captain John McBride. His commission for the East Indies, orders which had been publicly sent, were all a blind, and the real destination of the two ships was for a voyage of discovery in the South Seas. The jealousy of the Spaniards seemed to render the elaborate secrecy a necessary condition of success. No one on board the ships had a suspicion of what was before them till they had stood much further south than a passage to the Cape seemed to require. In passing through the Straits of Magellan they had frequent meetings with the Indians.

S.H. 447; S.G. 510.

Although Admiral John McBride is portrayed as a Naval Cartographer, this was only one aspect of a very distinguished Naval career. With the strong rumours of a French settlement, he commanded the second British expedition to the Falkland Islands in September, 1765, in the frigate "JASON", and it was he who discovered the French settlement at Port Louis in December, meeting de Nerville, the French Commander and giving him orders to leave or to swear allegiance to King George III. McBride was, perhaps, an unfortunate choice as leader of such an expedition. His interests were nautical, and it was from his gloomy reports that Dr. Johnson compiled his even gloomier appraisal of the Islands.

In August, 1767, Admiral McBride was appointed to H.M.S. "SEAFORD". Four years later, in 1771, he had two changes of command in one year. In 1776, he was appointed to the "BIENFAISANT" of 64 guns. It would seem that this was his first taste of action as he took part in the battle of Ushant on 27 July, 1778, which culminated in a court-martial in which he gave evidence strongly in favour of the Commander-in-Chief. In the later action off Cape St. Vincent in January, 1780, he played a very prominent part, receiving the surrender of one enemy vessel.

THE SPANISH ARRIVE

Thus both Britain and France had established small settlements in the 18th century, the French on East Falkland, the British on West Falkland. The Spanish authorities saw the Islands purely in the context of the Papal Bull, a piece of territory to which they were entitled and, in the climate of attempting to snatch maritime power, one from which every country, especially Britain, was to be excluded. The only use ever made of the Islands was as a penal settlement. It never was a colony for no woman ever lived there. In fact, they held the Islands in such contempt that no Governor could ever be persuaded to serve longer than his period of office, despite the inducement of double pay. To illustrate their feelings they changed the name of East Falkland to Soledad (solitude) and Port Louis became Port Soledad.

At first the Spaniards could not find the British settlement but, guided by two English deserters, in February, 1770, a Spanish commander arrived at Port Egmont to find not one frigate as he expected, but three: the "TAMAR", the "FAVOURITE" and the "SWIFT" and the storeship "FLORIDA". Confronted by a superior force the commander, Rubelcava, seeking desperately to find an escape from the situation, sent a communication ashore setting out his utter amazement at finding a British settlement "which was in violation of treaties which did not allow an intrusion into the King of Spain's domains." However, he offered an excuse that he would take no immediate action until he had received instructions from Madrid.

BRITISH FORCEFULLY EJECTED AND REINSTATED.

However, in June, 1770, encouraged by the discontent prevailing in the British Colonies in North America, and by assertions frequently made by the Opposition in Britain that the British Government was in no condition to go to war, and that the Government could be easily insulted, the authorities in Buenos Aires did not bother to wait for Royal instructions. The Governor immediately mounted an expedition of 1,600 soldiers and sailors to expel the one hundred British settlers by force. On 4 June, he appeared menacingly off Port Egmont in the frigate "INDUSTRIA" joined, two days later, by four more Spanish ships, some succeeding in entering the harbour pretending they only wanted water. Here they found that the entire defences were now just one frigate, the "FAVOURITE", commanded by Captain George Farmer. Ashore there were but a handful of soldiers with four small pieces of artillery.

S.H. 313; S.G. 389.

On 8 June, Captain Farmer, having taken what preventive arrangements could be achieved, sent the usual note instructing Madariaga, the Spanish commander, to leave. The Spaniards, in turn, called for the British to leave, and on a refusal, the commander was invited to visit the Spanish forces. An officer returned with the news that the Spanish force did mount to some 1,600 men. Captain Farmer still did not leave or yield, so the Spanish commander put his troops ashore. Although token shots were exchanged, defence of the British settlement was impossible. Captain Farmer surrendered, but the British "FAVOURITE" was deliberately delayed from returning to England until news of the surrender reached Buenos Aires and Spain.

The British Government were in a serious dilemma and were on the brink of war with Spain again but they were in no state of readiness, and the entire affair could end in embarrassment. Equally, the actions of the Spanish had been a flagrant act of antagonism and could not be dismissed. After some lengthy and acrimonious negotiations during which France refused to support Spain, it was agreed that Britain should re-occupy Port Egmont.

WITHDRAWAL BUT SOVEREIGNTY RETAINED.

On 15 September, 1771, at Port Egmont the Spanish officer in command formally relinquished the settlement to Captain Scott commanding the frigate "JUNO", the sloop "HOUND" and the storeship "FLORIDA". From that day Britain has regarded the Falkland Islands as her own by right of discovery. However, three years later the British abandoned the settlement in the name of economy but, in accordance with international law, left a metal plaque stating that their departure did not indicate a withdrawal of British Sovereignty: "Be it known unto all nations that the Falkland Islands, with this fort, storehouse, wharfs, bays and creeks there unto belonging, are sole property of His Most Sacred Majesty, George the Third, King of Great Britain, France, and Ireland, Defender of the Faith. In witness thereof this plate is set up, and His Britannic Majesty's colours left flying as a mark of possession by S.W.Clayton, Commanding Officer at Falkland's Islands, A.D. 1774."

Port Egmont soon deteriorated and in 1775, when the Spanish visited the site they found everything in a state of dilapidation and decay.

International laws change periodically, as do all laws, but the overwhelming opinion at that time was that a break in administration or entitlement did not affect sovereignty; there can be no loss of territory unless an intention to abandon has been declared and, in leaving behind a plaque claiming possession, the British did exactly the opposite.

ABANDONED BY SPAIN NEVER TO RETURN

In 1806 occurred the war with Buenos Aires and the so-called Falklands Governor, Juan Cristone Martinez, ordered by his Government, abandoned the Falkland Islands and fled to Montevideo, not Buenos Aires. Four years later, with the revolution resulting in the complete disintegration of the Spanish South American Empire, there was no return. Thus the Falkland Islands were abandoned by Spain, but NOT formally by Britain as already stated. Now faced with the rebellion in Buenos Aires, the Spanish Governor, having fled to Montevideo, the Province of Buenos Aires declared independence on 25 May, 1810, and what authority Spain had in South America had been transferred to Montevideo. Thus came into existence the United Provinces of La Plata, including all the settlements along the River Plate; Argentina as we know it today, did NOT exist; everything south and inland was empty pampas populated by wild cattle, horses and Indians, who were brutally exterminated forty years later in the Indian wars of General Urquiza. Thus the Falkland Islands, from 1806-1820, fourteen years, were completely abandoned by authority and became a haven for sealers.

Argentina's claim to the Falkland Islands is basically threefold: the first is geographical; the second is based on the Papal Decrees which had long been invalidated; the third is that she considers herself successor to Spain. If there is substance to this, it is Uruguay which has a claim, as Puerto Soledad was administered from Montevideo, not Buenos Aires, and there have been occasions at the United Nations when the Uruguayan delegate has reminded Argentina of this fact.

S.H. 47 B.A. T.
S.G. 46 B.A.T.

THE LAWLESS YEARS

On 1 November, 1820, Captain J.Weddell was at anchor in the "JANE" in Berkeley Sound when he was joined by a battered frigate, the "HEROIANA". Weddell was invited aboard, the Commander, Daniel Jewett, receiving him cordially. Weddell soon came to the opinion that Jewitt's chief concern in putting into the Islands was to refresh his crew, already stricken with scurvy, and that taking possession was an after-thought. This view was later confirmed by circumstances. The United Provinces of La Plata were more like the un-United Provinces, being in a state of unrest. There was no overall Government. Opinions expressed by some Argentinian historians refer to 1820 as 'the terrible year', the most anarchial year in Argentine's early history, there having been no fewer than 24 governments!! It is quite unthinkable that any of these governing bodies during their brief term of office could have had time to think about the Falklands let alone despatch Jewett to take possession. There had been some French naturalists, the de Freycinets, in the Islands and they had brought news to Montevideo. It was on this hearsay that Jewett had personally acted, taking formal possession on 6 November, an act later confirmed by the Buenos Aires Government.

THE "HEROINANA"

LOUIS VERNET

However, by 1823, the potential value of increasing cattle had been recognised when the United Provinces Government offered the fishing and cattle rights to Louis Vernet and Jorge Pacheco. Louis Vernet, a merchant of Hamburg, of French birth but South American naturalisation, was granted a considerable acreage of land, together with the fishing and cattle rights of East Falkland. He had grandiose plans for creating 'a great national fishery'. However, the only attempt at commercial fishing in the Islands was the small effort from 1826 to 1831 by Vernet, and it is recorded that in 1829 he salted down and exported to Brazil a considerable tonnage, mainly grey mullet. Some line fishing for rock cod also played its part in Vernet's business. His attempts at founding a 'great national fishery' ended. To this day, however, in camp settlements, 'fish walls' are used extensively, a system which has descended from Vernet's operations. At this time also a decree claiming sovereignty over the Falkland Islands was made by the Buenos Aires Government, to which the British protested as not being in accordance with British rights of discovery and sovereignty not ruled out by our withdrawal in 1774.

LOUIS VERNET

Tensions were running high among the American sealers and, at one stage, even the American Government took a hand, stating that because the U.S.A. was once a colony of Britain, she had now inherited the right to seal in the Falklands. Perhaps this stirred the United Provinces to resurrect a claim on a similar basis; they went one stage further, not only reiterating their proximity but issued a decree to the effect that the Islands were geologically allied to South America. Britain protested vigorously, reminding all of their rights of discovery, the marks of possession left there and that all formalities had been observed for the intention to renew occupation. Modern techniques have established that geologically the Falkland Islands are more closely associated with South Africa, as a part of the huge breakaway continent of Gondwanaland, than South America.

THE LEXINGTON'S REVENGE

At one time Vernet attempted to prevent sealing operations by foreign vessels, with little success, so he 'arrested' three United States schooners, the master of one being taken to Buenos Aires for trial. The United States representative at that time was a somewhat volatile person who, acting on his own initiative and with the collusion of the commander of the U.S. corvette "LEXINGTON", Sylas Duncan, took revenge by physically destroying the Port Soledad settlement, proclaiming the Islands free of all government. This action was upheld by the United States Government itself, in the firm belief that American sealers still had the right to fish those waters, that inheritance arising from the United States once being a British colony. Another early Antarctic explorer, Captain Matthew Brisbane, who had been left in charge by Vernet, was treated as a pirate, clapped in irons and taken to Montevideo.

Absent from the Colony when the "LEXINGTON" took revenge, Vernet never returned to the Islands. He made several applications to obtain compensation from the British Government for stock and produce left behind which had subsequently come under British care with the return of British rule in 1833. A miserly sum was granted some twenty six years after he left the Islands.

BRITISH RIGHTS RE-ASSERTED

A temporary Spanish Governor was murdered by a gang of mutineers, and Captain Onslow in H.M.S. "CLIO" arrived in December, 1832 to reclaim British sovereignty through discovery. He handed the following note to the Captain of the "SARANDI", Jose Pinedo, who had taken over following the murder of the Spanish Governor:

"Sir, I have to acquaint you that I have received directions from his Excellency, the Commander-in-Chief of His Britannic Majesty's ships and vessels of war, South American station, in the name of His Britannic Majesty, to exercise the 'rights of sovereignty over these Islands'. It is my intention to hoist, tomorrow morning, the national flag of Great Britain on shore, when I request you will be pleased to hoist down your flag on shore, and withdraw your forces, taking with you all stores, etc., belonging to your Government. I am, sir, Your most Obedient servant, John James Onslow, Commander."

Then, on 3 January, 1833, three boats manned by seamen and marines put off from the "CLIO" and landed in the little harbour of Port Louis. Those personnel from the Provinces of Buenos Aires invited to leave, together with twenty-five soldiers who had arrived on the schooner "SARANDI", eventually sailed on 5 January with any other person who had voluntarily wished to leave.

S.H. 378 S.G. 439.

To-day Argentina likes to stress that Buenos Aires settlers were ousted and replaced. Like so many other statements, this is completely incorrect: only those who wished to leave did so, the remainder continuing under British rule at the re-named Port Louis. In fact, very few settlers came from the country that was to become Argentina but mostly from the Banda Oriental (Uruguay).

A few days later Captain Onslow in H.M.S. "CLIO" sailed leaving William Dickson, the senior British resident in the Islands, in charge. Ever since that day, British Administration had flourished in those Islands except for those tragic months of 1982.

THE PORT LOUIS MURDERS

In the early 19th century many navigators sailed to southern waters and beyond, seeking more accurate information. One, perpetuated in many ways in the Falkland Islands, was Vice-Admiral Robert Fitzroy in command of H.M.S. "BEAGLE", with Charles Darwin aboard.

S.H. 449 S.G.512

Entering the Navy at 14, he became a Lieutenant at 20. In 1828 he was in command of the brig "BEAGLE" on a survey of the coasts of South America, stopping at the Falkland Islands in 1833 when Darwin both collected the flora and fauna of the Islands.

When the "BEAGLE" entered Berkeley Sound and found Port Louis, both Captain Fitzroy and Charles Darwin were dismayed at the state of what appeared almost a ruined settlement in which sealers, whalers and gauchos, having tasted freedom, were taking full advantage. During this visit Captain Brisbane, who had been carried off by the U.S. "LEXINGTON" as a 'pirate', returned to take charge of the settlement. Captain Fitzroy described Brisbane, Dickson and another British settler, Captain William Lowe, as the handful of honest settlers whose conduct shone out in contrast to the others.

S.H. 349; S.G. 425

S.H. 348; S.G. 424.

One of the fascinating things about Darwin is that he really does seem to have been one of those men whose career quite unexpectedly is decided for them by a single stroke of fortune. On the Falkland Islands he recorded a curious fox, or Warrah, which lived there in great numbers. He made notes that penguins used their wings as fins, some geese theirs as paddles. He never went to sea again, partly because of his seasickness, and finally died at the age of 73.

S.H. 346; S.G. 422

Darwin made collections of many hundreds of specimens of plants, birds, fish, insects and other invertebrates, rocks and fossils, most of which still exist. He also noted that the unique, strikingly tame Warrah or Falkland Fox had by the time of his visit been reduced in numbers. He noted that they were easily killed by a gaucho holding a piece of meat in one hand and a knife in the other. The grass was set on fire and often they could be seen running to seek other quarters. The last Falkland Fox was killed at Shallow Bay, West Falkland, in 1876, well within Darwin's lifetime.

Captain Brisbane attempted to restore Vernet's business and create law and order in the community, a very demanding and somewhat dangerous course to follow, as much of Vernet's labour force were Indian convicts who, having enjoyed relative freedom, were unwilling to return to a lawful state. The fuse of an explosive situation is said to have been lit by not having a suitable currency with which to pay the men so, secretly plotting against Brisbane, five of the convicts and three gauchos took their chance on 26 August, 1833 when Captain Lowe had already left with four others to go sealing. They attacked and murdered Brisbane, Anton Wagner, a German settler; and Don Ventura Pasos. Their graves can still be seen at Port Louis. All but one of the other settlers (13 men, 3 women and 2 children) escaped to Turf Island in Berkeley Sound on 29 August, where they remained until help arrived some months later.

It had been decided after the visit of H.M.S. "CLIO" that a regular visit would be made to the Islands by Royal Navy vessels, so on hearing of the murders, H.M.S. "CHALLENGER" set off from Rio de Janeiro to arrive at Port Louis on 9 January, 1834. The following day Lt. Smith was installed as Governor, and his first task was to apprehend the murderers.

Successfully achieved, the ringleader, Rivero, and others were sent to Britain for trial. In Argentina Rivero was hailed as a hero and during the occupation of 1982, they changed the name of Stanley for a time to Puerto Rivero, named after this heartless killer. As for Captain Brisbane, who at the time of the arrival of H.M.S. "CLIO" was in Buenos Aires, helping the Government there in its complicated wrangle with the Government of the United States of America after the "LEXINGTON" destruction, he is still depicted as a symbol of Britain which 'seized the Islands in January, 1833.'

THE MOVE TO STANLEY

For the following eight years (1834-1842) supervision was carried out by superintendents and a small naval party to help keep law and order and to exercise some administrative duties. However, in 1841, Richard C. Moody, aged 28, was appointed Lt. Governor and ordered to proceed to the Islands to carry out primary colonisation. He sailed in the "HEBE" with some more settlers, arriving at Port Louis 13 January, 1842, and by June, 1843, was officially appointed Governor and Commander-in-Chief of the settlement and Dependencies. Moody formed a favourable impression of the Islands and of their future, firmly of the opinion that they could survive on their own natural resources; but he lacked financial support from the British Government.

S.H. 269; S.G. 345a

As for the 189-ton brig "HEBE", under the command of Captain C.F. Anderson, she was originally built at Poole in 1829 but was restored and thoroughly repaired in 1841, being yellow-sheathed in 1844. Registered in London, she called at nine to ten monthly intervals with merchandise and supplies from England and from 1846 often carried the mail.

S.H. 50 B.A.T.
S.G. 49 B.A.T.

Following some careful examinations and reports on various sites for a new capital, in which Admiral Sulivan and another Antarctic explorer, Sir James Clark Ross, gave influential advice, work finally commenced to move from Port Louis to the narrow and sharply rising strip of land forming the southern shore of Jackson's Harbour, the inner deep water harbour of Port William. Officially the town came into being on 18 July, 1845. Currently titled 'STANLEY', the prefix 'PORT' refers to the harbour although the name 'PORT STANLEY' is commonly used for the town. It was, of course, named after Lord Stanley. The settlement then comprised 24 turf houses and about 100 inhabitants, most of them sealers and whalers.

S.H. 450; S.G. 513.

Probably the least known of all Naval personnel is Admiral and hydrographer Sir Bartholomew James Sulivan, yet he had long and lasting connections with the Falkland Islands. In 1837 he was posted to the "ARROW" and sent to survey the Islands. His wife accompanied him, and the Christian name Falkland given to his eldest son marks the family belief that he was the first British subject born in the Islands. In 1842, he returned to the Falklands in the brig "PHILOMEL" (a very familiar Islands name). Towards the end of 1848 he obtained three years leave of absence and went with his family to live in the Falklands until 1851.

On his way home in a merchant vessel the crew mutinied, and until they were starved into submission, the Captain, the mate and Sulivan worked the ship going aloft and bringing her under easy sail as a timely precaution. After a passage of 90 days they arrived at Liverpool. On the imminence of war with Russia at the beginning of 1854, Sulivan applied for a command; but his reputation as a surveying officer stood in his way. In this capacity he eventually served in the Baltic during the campaigns of 1854 and 1855.

Indeed Stanley could not have become a port at a better time. The Peruvian guano trade was in full swing, whilst a possibly greater attraction was the discovery of gold in California in 1848 and 1850 in Australia. Rounding The Horn became an occupational hazard as there was of yet no Panama Canal. Thus Stanley became an excellent place at which to take aboard fresh provisions. However, in trying to make the Islands, some came to grief on the rocky shore and being too broken to repair, were condemned and sold as hulks in Stanley. Thus came into being not only a ship repairing industry, but also the 'wrecking trade', a trade in vessels accidentally or otherwise wrecked on the shores of the Islands.

S.G. 381; S.G. 442.

Governor Moody's successor, Governor George Rennie, became somewhat concerned over the wrong type of person entering the Colony as a settler. In answer to his request to London he was informed he would receive more Royal Marines accompanied by 30 Army pensioners with their wives and families. They were by no means the red-coated elderly gentlemen one associates these days with Chelsea pensioners, for the average age was 42, the youngest being in his 20s and the eldest only slightly over 50. However, a pioneering life demanded much more than barrack life, and some could not stand the strain. Seven families left, five staying in the Islands to become excellent craftsmen and tradesmen. Many of their descendants form part of the present population.

S.H. 379; S.G. 440.

In 1854 wages in the trade had reached the high level of 25 shillings per day and prices soared accordingly. As the ship repair trade was on a fairly casual basis anyway with the few facilities that were available, some ships were kept waiting weeks or even months. The peak was reached in 1867 when ship repairers had a novel way of securing trade. Each kept a man permanently posted on a vantage point on the heights above the town, whose job it was to keep a lookout for disabled ships making towards the Islands, and as soon as one was sighted the firm's rowing boat would put out. On the appointment of a Government pilot, a lookout was erected on the signal staff and the

S.H. 188; S.G. 259.

sighting of vessels became his responsibility. Labour was always in short supply because as soon as artisans had made a little money they would be off to England with their families; £500 was not an unusual amount for the thrifty man to take home with him after five years in Stanley.

THE S.S."GREAT BRITAIN"

Probably the most famous hulk of all in the Islands was the S.S. "GREAT BRITAIN", launched at Bristol in July, 1843, the largest ship in the world at that time, considered a marvel of engineering and designed by Brunel. There were very few ships in being over 1,000 tons, yet the "GREAT BRITAIN" was almost 3,500 tons. She was also the first with screw propulsion. Her maiden voyage was from Liverpool to New York on 26 July, 1845 and is believed to have taken just fifteen days. Her Atlantic service was short lived for in September, 1846, she ran aground in Dundrum Bay, Ireland, and on being refloated sold for the Australian emigrant trade, the first of 32 such voyages over a period of 25 years.

S.H. 115; S.G. 185

She saw good service as a troop carrier during the Indian Mutiny and the Crimean War before once again being sold, embarking on the savage route round The Horn to San Francisco. Suffering damage on one trip from South Wales her cargo of coal caught fire, so she ran for Stanley, arriving on 25 May, 1886. Condemned as too costly to repair her sailing days were over but not her career. For another 47 years, until 1933, she was used by the Falkland Islands Co. as a storage hulk and then regretfully had to be abandoned. After an aborted proposal to sink her she was granted honourable retirement in Sparrow Cove.

S.H. 468; S.G. 530.

However, there were other surprises for the 'grand old lady', for on 6 April, 1970, she floated again. Many Falklanders would have said the project to return her to the U.K. was madness; others said the hulk should not leave, but leave she did creating the longest maritime tow in history, and she is now being fully restored at her launching place of Bristol. The S.S. "GREAT BRITAIN" was not only a famous vessel in her own right, but one which had survived the longest life of an iron ship ever built and which came of a celebrated line.

THE "JHELUM"

A silent memorial to those mainly engaged in the guano trade is the "JHELUM", launched by Joseph Steel and Son at Liverpool on 24 May, 1849, in their own shipyard and on their own account, for the combination of merchant shipowner and shipbuilder was not uncommon at that time. In 1863 she was sold to Joseph Conrad and James Wilson also of Liverpool who, in turn, sold her to Matthew Wilson and five months later to

S.H. 343; S.G. 419.

G.J. Widdicombe and C.R. Bell her final owner, again from Liverpool. Although described as an East Indiaman, her sailings were mainly to South America.

Guano was often the return cargo, an exceedingly unpleasant substance, being very rich in ammonia and highly corrosive to ship's metalwork and very bad for the health of the crew. On the outward journeys she appears to have taken between 100 and 120 days, and on return journeys between 90 and 100 days. However, we do know that her principal loading ports were small isolated anchorages in Peru and Chile, and the commodities loaded were either guano, nitrates or copper. It was on one such return voyage that she met some exceedingly rough weather around The Horn and was subsequently quite heavily damaged, far too costly to repair, thus being sold in Stanley, where she rests to this day, as a hulk of the Falkland Islands Government.

THE "LADY ELIZABETH"

Another well known hulk in Stanley is that of the "LADY ELIZABETH", launched in June, 1879, by Sunderland ship builder Robert Thompson Jnr., at his Southwick yard. She was an iron barque of 1,208 tons gross and 1,155 tons net. She was 223ft. long, 35ft. wide with a depth of hold 21ft. 4". Built for London shipowner John Wilson, she was first registered at the Port of London on 21 August, 1879, and was the largest of that fleet. She had many different owners before finally being sold to a Norwegian company in 1906. The "LADY ELIZABETH" sailed on her last voyage on 4 December, 1912, with lumber from Vancouver for Delagoa Bay in Southern Mozambique. Passing down the Pacific, she was not reported until arriving at Stanley in distress on 14 March, 1913.

S.H. 341; S.G. 417.

The "LADY ELIZABETH" had encountered bad weather and had lost four men overboard; also two boats and part of her deck cargo as well as damage to the wheel, rigging, bulwarks and deck fittings. Finally, two days prior to her arrival, she struck the Uranie Rocks off Volunteer Point about 15 miles north east of Stanley, sustaining a 6ft. break in her keel and a foot long hole in her bottom. After examination she was condemned early in June, 1913, rather than face the cost of repairs in Stanley. Finally, on 17 February, 1936, during a particularly fierce gale, she broke from her moorings, and drifted east across the harbour, and went aground in Whalebone Cove near Stanley Airport where she lies today.

BISHOP STIRLING, CHRISTCHURCH CATHEDRAL AND KEPPEL ISLAND

One will always associate Christian worship with Bishop Stirling and his missionary work among the Indians of South America. Born at Kingston-on-Thames, he was educated at Exeter College, Oxford, taking his degree in 1852. Five years later he joined the Patagonian Missionary Society, working for five years before applying to be sent to the Falkland Islands as Superintendent of the Mission Station on Keppel Island, finally arriving on 30 January, 1863. It was to this man living in a small wooden house in

S.H. 181; S.G. 252.

Tierra del Fuego at the time that the "ALLEN GARDINER" returned in August, 1869, bringing a summons for him to return to England as soon as possible for his consecration as Bishop of the Falkland Islands. He eventually returned in November, receiving an Hon. D.D. degree at Oxford, and becoming consecrated Bishop in Westminster Abbey on 21 December, 1869.

An indefatigable worker with tireless energy, his Pastoral was a review of his work during his 30 years as Bishop, and although much had been accomplished he still regretted the failure of some projects through one cause or another of which the death of his first wife had a profound effect. Soon afterwards he resigned, but not to rest, for in 1901 he was appointed Canon of Wells. On his 90th birthday, January, 1919, a peel was rung on the Cathedral bells in his honour. Finally he entered retirement in September, 1920. These were the characteristics of the man which have been stressed over and over again, and which were a very present part of him to the day of his death, 19 November, 1923, he being laid to rest in Wells Cathedral.

When in 1863 the Rev. W.H. Stirling became the new Superintendent of the Keppel Island Mission Station, he found, despite the massacre of a previous party on the South American mainland, a family of Yahgan Indians. Their presence was important, as through them they became well versed in the language and eventually a Yamana-English Dictionary of 32,000 words was compiled. Soon after his arrival Stirling accompanied a Thomas Bridges and the Yahgan Indians to the mainland. Rather apprehensive of their reception, all worries were allayed when Bridges talked with them in their own tongue explaining they had only come to help. Many Fuegians wished to visit Keppel, and although a new mission station was set up at Ushuaia in 1869, Keppel remained its headquarters. Finally the Mission Station, continuing until 1869, moved to the South American continent, and Keppel Island was eventually sold to Dean Brothers of Pebble Island; but it has at least been preserved as an integral part of Falkland Islands history.

S.H. 315; S.G. 391.

Church life in Stanley in 1844 centred on a small room of the military barracks in the dockyard. From here a building on the site of the present Speedwell Store, John Street, followed by part of the exchange Building (which was called Holy Trinity Church) on the site of the Cathedral, and finally a disused sail loft, were used in turn for Church Services. However, following heavy rain and a serious peat slip, Holy Trinity Church was damaged beyond repair, so an appeal was launched for a new building. The sum of £6,000 was the target of which Bishop Stirling promised to raise half, and this was very soon achieved. Materials were bought in England, some being brought out on the "LADY ELIZABETH". The foundation stone was laid by Governor Kerr on 21 February, 1892. It was Bishop Stirling's concern to provide a sanctuary for sailors, a Parish Church for the community and a Cathedral Church for a vast diocese. Christchurch Cathedral is that building, and is much

S.H. 179; S.G. 250.

S.H. 180; S.G. 251.

beautified by two handsome memorials to his life's work in the Diocese of the Falkland Islands. Christchurch Cathedral has recently commemorated its Centenary, (1992) with a refurbishment, the bricks for which were made in Berkshire and the new stained glass at Horsham in Sussex. The Archbishop of Canterbury, Dr. Carey, travelled to the Islands as the Bishop of the Falkland Islands, to re-consecrate the Cathedral in February, 1992.

WHALES AND WHALING

To symbolise what was once one of the main occupations of early settlers there has been erected on Arch Green, Port Stanley (a small park between the Falkland Islands Company store and Christchurch Cathedral presented to the Colony by the Company) the lower jaw bones of two sperm whales brought from South Georgia and presented to the Colony to mark its Centenary in 1933.

S.H. 76; S.G. 146.

By far the most important of the toothed whales is the Sperm Whale and, in appearance, it is one of the strangest creatures. Its body is roughly cylindrical, tapering away abruptly behind to the tail flukes. A fully grown bull is about twice as large as a fully grown cow and may reach the length of about 60ft. In this size difference it is the exact opposite to another type of whale, the Baleen. The principle grounds and feeding areas are in tropical and sub-tropical seas, and it forms a high proportion of the catches of stations where whaling is still continued. The diet is mainly squid, many of them of quite enormous size. It is also polygamous, the cows roaming in the tropical oceans in 'harem bands' in the charge of one or more proprietor bulls or 'schoolmasters'. The name 'sperm' refers to the waxy substance which it carries in a reservoir in its head, the function being to increase the buoyancy of the head.

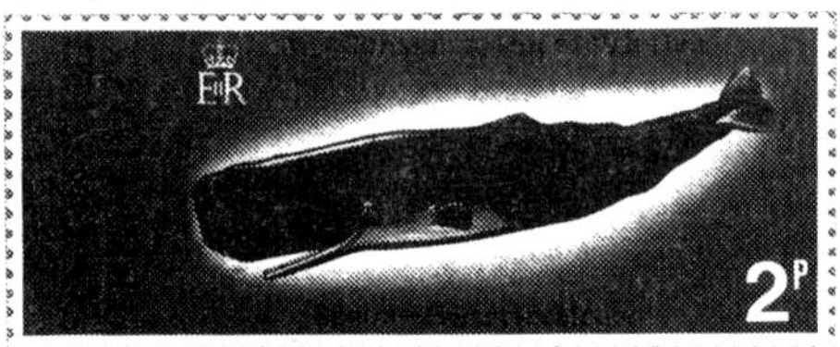

S.H. 79 B.A.T. S.G. 79 B.A.T.

There are six species of Baleen Whales, the largest and most valuable being the Blue Whale. It is a majestic animal, the largest living creature on earth, where a fully grown cow may reach the length of 100ft., about that of a three car electric train. The height in the middle is about 20ft., roughly that of a train. They break surface three to five times at half minute intervals, after which they disappear in deep dives of up to ten minutes. Basically they are slate-blue in colour all over except for the undersides of the flippers which are white. They tend to travel in small groups of up to half a dozen known as 'schools'. They strain out of the water large

S.H. 523 S.G. 586

quantities of minute food too small to be pursued, caught and devoured by teeth. They filter this planktonic food by means of a series of triangular flexible plates made of a horny substance called 'whalebone' hanging down from the upper jaw, with only an inch or two between them. The inner edges of this whalebone are frayed out to form a mat of coarse hair over the roof of the mouth. On this the planktonic food becomes entangled. The water is forced out and the food swept back into the throat with the aid of the tongue.

S.H. 238; S.G. 313.

However, whaling is all but finished in these southern waters, and seals are also now a fully protected animal. It was hardly apt, therefore, that the official Coat-of-Arms should embody a seal in its design, and a new Coat-of-Arms was required which reflected more the economy of the Islands. Thus in layman's language, the present Coat-of-Arms forms a shield that is divided horizontally by a wavy line. The upper half of the shield is blue, with a depiction of a ram in its natural colours standing on grass. The lower half of the shield is white, with two wavy bars as a depiction of the ship "DESIRE" in gold with red crosses on its flag and pennons, and the mainsail having on it five wavy-rayed red stars. The motto "DESIRE THE RIGHT" remains as before.

SHEEP FARMING

In the early days the economy had been based on sealing and whaling, much of it completely unrestricted. Then the economy turned to killing the herds of wild cattle that roamed East Falkland, but when these had been over slaughtered the economy turned to sheep farming, possibly the first attempt on a small scale as far back as 1840, even before the arrival of Governor Moody. After more than its fair share of setbacks through wide ranging problems, much of its present day success has been due to learning the hard way and establishing, through trial and error, the right breed of sheep, now almost entirely Corriedale, Polwarth and Romney. Unsuccessful attempts were made to export mutton, but it is high quality wool fleeces which predominate. Since 1982 a radical change has occurred in that now almost all farms are no longer ranched by companies based in Britain, but have been subdivided and owned and farmed by Falkland Islanders.

S.H. 102; S.G. 172.

THE DEFENCE FORCE

There are three more events which occurred in the nineteenth century which should be recorded; the first is that the Federal Republic of Argentina was finally established in 1853, twenty years after the British had returned to the Falkland Islands to restore law and order in 1833. The second is that in 1858, during the Crimean War, a short lived and temporary defence force evolved when some eighty men volunteered. That was the embryo stage of a permanent force formed in 1892 and known as the Falkland Islands Volunteers Corps. To-day it is the Falkland Islands Defence Force, which has played a major part in all subsequent alarms and excursions. In fact, there was a further alarm in 1892 when a Chilean steamer belonging to the Revolutionary Party with some 200 armed soldiers as well as sailors aboard requested permission to enter Port William for engine repairs. The third was that from 1881, the Falkland Islands, having been grant aided since 1833, finally became financially independent.

The principal object of the Volunteer Ordinance subsequently introduced was to provide for an organised Volunteer Force and to legalise a Capitation Grant. The Bill was framed on the basis of the Volunteer Ordinance in force in the Straits Settlements. On 13 June, 1892, 37 Volunteers were sworn in at Government House as a first instalment of the Force. The uniforms were to be made of stout grey serge to the colour of the British Volunteer Corps of Great Britain.

The name was only changed to its present title after the commencement of the First World War, when the entire Colony was placed upon a war footing. Indeed, some of the ill-fated vessels of Admiral Cradock's fleet sailed from the Islands to suffer defeat from a numerically superior force at the Battle of Coronel. At this time, too, some artillery guns were stationed at vulnerable points on the Islands. Many civilians also joined up and were, of course, subject to Volunteer Active Service Ordinance. In the early part of the war, during December, by order from Executive Council, all public houses were closed for some time, for "the further efficiency of the defence force". But this does not appear to have lasted very long. Eight members of the Corps were accidentally drowned in a boat accident on 1 December, 1916. On the concentration of the German Squadron off the West Coast of South America, the corps constructed a barricade of peat reinforced with timber around the Wireless Telegraphy Station at the suggestion of the O.C. H.M.S. "GOOD HOPE", before that squadron, under Admiral Cradock, departed to seek the enemy. Also a field gun and further small arms were put ashore from H.M.S. "CANOPUS", a large warship which was unable to sail with Cradock.

S.H. 183;
S.G. 254.

There were now strict regulations covering the harbour and Port William, especially for the arrival and entry of ships. In November over 600 women and children were evacuated to settlements in different parts of the Colony. The gun batteries came under the tuition of an instructor left by H.M.S. "INVINCIBLE", the volunteer crews rapidly gaining a knowledge of the drill and manipulation, taking over full control and operation when the naval servicemen and instructors left in 1915. During this year also, Falkland Islanders were beginning to go to Britain to join the Forces, ten direct from the islands, seven of whom were actually serving volunteers. Those who gave their lives in addition to the eight drowned, totalled ten, making a final Roll of Honour of 18. Now, too, the uniform was changed to new khaki dress and this was regarded as a great improvement.

S.H.185
S.G. 256.

Two 6" naval guns were landed in 1917, one being set up at Sparrow Cove and one in Stanley itself. The first was later dragged to Mt. Lowe and the second to Sappers Hill. There the guns remained though they were, of course, serviced and kept operational until in the 1930s H.M.S. "DURBAN" moved the Mt. Lowe gun to Sappers Hill and the other was moved to Canopus Hill. During the 1939-45 war, when the 11th Battalion of the West Yorkshire Regiment was in Stanley on garrison duty, they moved the Sappers Hill gun to Canopus Hill and both guns are there to this day, though out of active use. Finally, the Defence Force is still very much in evidence to-day, having been closely involved in the tragic days of 1982, and thankfully now returned to the more mundane work of ceremonials and state occasions: but a very well worthwhile force.

S.H. 184 S.G. 255.

BATTLE OF THE FALKLAND ISLANDS, 1914

It is not so well known that the Falkland Islands have played a major part in the gaining of supremacy of the seas in both World Wars. It was on the morning of 8 December, 1914, that an observer of the Falkland Islands Defence Force spotted the German Pacific Fleet approaching, and H.M.S. "GLASGOW" fired a gun to draw attention to the signal flying from the masthead of H.M.S. "CANOPUS": "Enemy in sight". Thus began the Battle of the Falkland Islands which was to secure British supremacy of the seas in the South Atlantic for the rest of the First World War, with the eventual complete destruction of the German fleet. The 8 December, 1914, became an important date in local history and is still commemorated by an annual holiday. The German Squadron was composed of five ships:
the "GNEISENAU",
the "NURNBERG",
the "SCHARNHORST",
the "LEIPZIG" and
the "DRESDEN" with the "BADEN" and "ST. ISABEL" as transports. The British Squadron comprised seven vessels including two battle cruisers:
H.M.S. "INVINCIBLE",
H.M.S. "INFLEXIBLE", and the cruisers H.M.S. "KENT",
H.M.S. "GLASGOW",

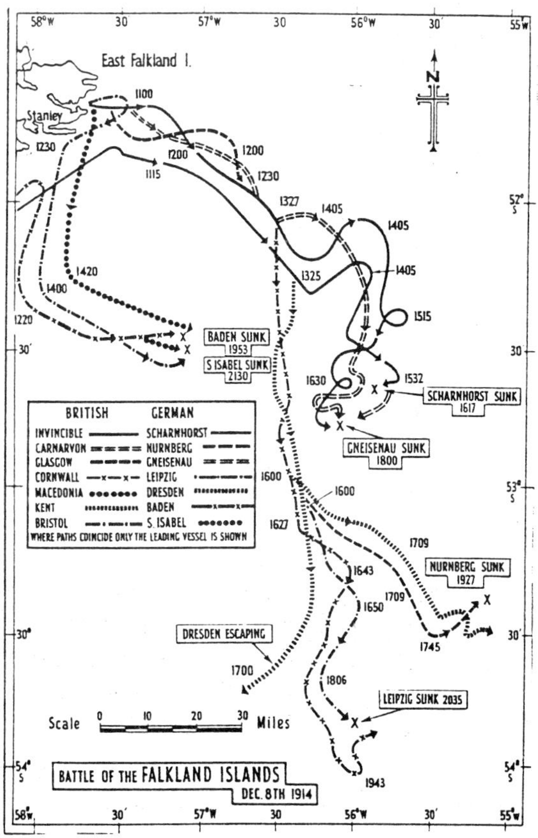

H.M.S. "CARNARVON", H.M.S. "CORNWALL" and H.M.S. "BRISTOL". It had been formed and despatched to the Islands following a defeat at Coronel and arrived in the Islands only on the 7 December.

Once battle was joined it appeared to be divided into two separate actions, with H.M.S. "GLASGOW", H.M.S. "CORNWALL" and H.M.S. "KENT" pursuing the now fleeing "DRESDEN", "LEIPZIG" and "NURNBERG". H.M.S. "GLASGOW" was to starboard to engage the "DRESDEN" and in a running fight which continued for an hour before the range dropped to 9000 yards, H.M.S. "GLASGOW" was hit twice, damaging one of her boilers and causing her to lose speed. Consequently she had no chance of locating the fleeing "DRESDEN" which made her escape in the mist and under cover of night. The "GLASGOW" suffered no further damage or casualties. She now joined H.M.S. "CORNWALL" in finishing off the "LEIPZIG" and subsequently rescuing survivors, but between them they only picked up seven officers and eleven men. H.M.S. "GLASGOW" suffered few casualties -- - one dead and four wounded. However, the "DRESDEN" had only temporarily escaped, for she was eventually hunted down by H.M.S. "KENT" after weeks of searching and was sunk.

S.H. 145; S.G. 215.

The "NURNBERG" opened fire first and the "KENT" replied. The German gunfire was extremely accurate, but despite this the "KENT" closed to within 3,000 yards and saw her own shells bursting all over the "NURNBERG". By 18.30 she had practically stopped and she ceased firing, but as it was observed she was still flying her colours and did not appear to be sinking, the "KENT" opened fire again. Five minutes later she lowered her colours. The German vessel was now sinking fast and at 19.26 she heeled over and slowly sank. The "KENT" did her utmost to save life, but regretfully only twelve were picked up and five of these died. Von Spee's son was not amongst those rescued. The "KENT" had been struck 38 times, but there was no serious damage to the ship.

S.H. 146; S.G. 216.

H.M.S. "INVINCIBLE" and H.M.S. "INFLEXIBLE", supported by H.M.S. "CARNARVON" engaged the "SCHARNHORST" and "GNEISENAU" at a range of about 13,500 yards. The German gunfire was excellent and took some effect on "INVINCIBLE", but the "SCHARNHORST" also suffered. Now began manoeuvres to gain a better position until guns could open up again at a range of 10,000 yards. The German fire was so effective that Sturdee swung his ships through 32 points to clear the smoke which fouled the range; but the "SCHARNHORST" was badly holed fore and aft below the waterline so that she was drawing 3ft. more than usual, and she could be seen to be on fire in several places. By 15.30 her third funnel had been shot away and her gunfire had slackened perceptibly. Indeed, so many of the German's guns on their engaged

S.H. 147; S.G. 217.

side had been put out of action that Von Spee swung his ships 10 points to starboard in order to bring other broadsides to bear. But this move allowed Sturdee to gain the lee position, and now the "INVINCIBLE" and "INFLEXIBLE" had changed targets. Almost immediately the "SCHARNHORST" sank, leaving the "GNEISENAU" alone. She was too badly damaged to effect an escape and, with all three British cruisers concentrating upon her, and blazing furiously, the end was in sight. The flag flying at the fore-truck was apparently hauled down, but the flag at the peak continued flying. At 17.50 the “Cease fire” was made. The "GNEISENAU" had expended all her ammunition, lost steam from all her boilers and had some 600 of her crew killed or wounded. Orders had been given to scuttle the ship. The "INVINCIBLE" lost no man killed or wounded although struck by 22 shells.

S.H. 148;
S.G. 218.

The Battle of the Falkland Islands, 8 December, 1914, was over. The fact that the Islands had been saved from a potential occupation by an enemy power was as much attributable to the calm, unhurried way with which Admiral Sturdee faced a potentially dangerous situation as to the superiority of his squadron over that of the enemy. This memorable victory is still commemorated not only by the 8 December being a general public holiday throughout the Islands, but also by the imposing memorial just beyond Government House on Ross Road, erected by grateful Islanders as a tribute to all those gallant men, especially those who gave their lives.

The end of the German cruiser "Dresden".

The final chapter had not quite been written, for the "DRESDEN" was still at large. It was not until 14 March, 1915, that she was finally found in Cumberland Bay on the West Coast of South America. She was already in an appalling state, and quickly hoisted the white flag, the crew leaving for the shore. She was actually blown up by her own skeleton crew and settled in those far away waters. Thus the entire German Pacific Fleet had now been sunk.

INTERNAL MAIL AND TRANSPORT

In 1978, the Stamp Committee in the Islands accepted the idea of commemorating the first Falkland Islands postage stamp by the inclusion of the first four stamps in the design of a set, but they insisted that the early Post Offices should be depicted --- the First and Second Stanley Post Offices, the First Fox Bay Post Office and that which once served on New Island. It was in 1878 that the Falkland Islands joined those countries which issued their own stamps, and so Falkland Islands' philately had begun. This second Stanley Post Office was burnt down in 1944, destroying a considerable quantity of the archives and handstamps.

S.H. 276; S.G. 352.

In 1883 Fox Bay became the port of entry for West Falkland, the first entries being made in 1884. For some years Fox Bay was engaged in the export of West Falkland produce direct to other countries, but compared with Port Stanley, it was but a minor port. One person acted as police constable and Customs Officer. In 1895 a Stipendiary Magistrate was appointed and he became Deputy Collector of Customs. In 1916, the importance of Fox Bay as a port came to an end. Today the Government Officer retained there issues clearance when required by vessels entering from abroad, but for many years this has not been necessary. The Post Office was opened in 1899.

S.H. 275; S.G. 351.

New Island had been the seat of various whaling undertakings for a few years, but it was not until 1908 that Messrs. Christian Salvesen of Leith commenced serious whaling following the issue of a lease on the site. A Post Office was accordingly opened at South Harbour and a Deputy Postmaster placed in charge. The officer, Arthur Kirwin, was appointed on 29 July, 1909, and his duties included Deputy Collector of Customs and Deputy Harbour Master. Later the same year he was additionally Deputy Shipping Master, when the Governor in Council declared South Harbour to be a Port of Entry in August, 1909. It finally closed on 1 June, 1917, never to open again, when Christian Salvesen moved their whaling operations and equipment to Leith Harbour in South Georgia.

S.H. 277; S.G. 353.

There have never been more than three Post Offices on the Islands, and for many years there were only two, Fox Bay and Stanley; but with the opening of Mount Pleasant Airport,

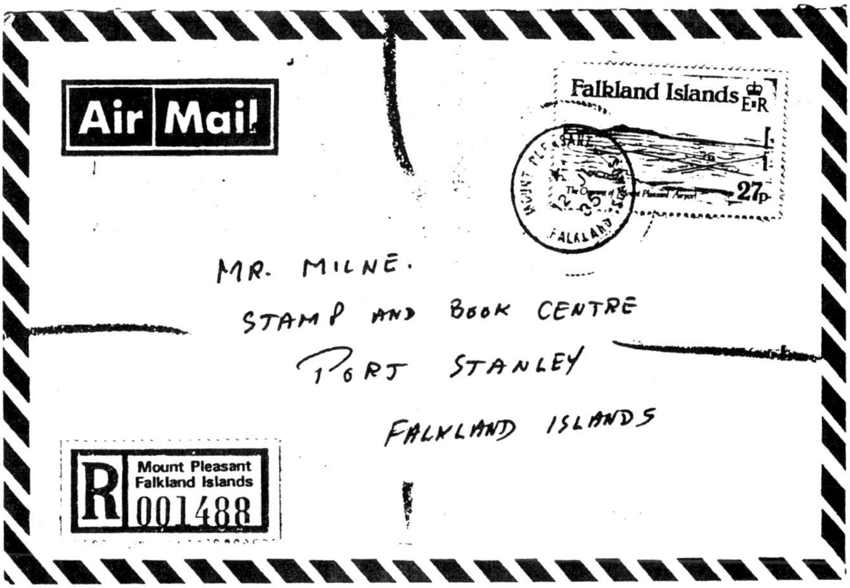

the number returned to three as there is now a fully operational Post Office at that site.

In those early days the only method of transport of both mails and materials was by horse. On West Falkland, the main port of entry being Fox Bay, the mail from beyond the Islands would first come and go via Stanley, thence by Island schooner to Fox Bay. It was only 60-70 years ago when six or seven mailmen and their 'cargueros' (from the gaucho word for load) would assemble at Fox Bay and, after transfer of mails and loads, fan out in their various directions for their home stations. Before the days of telephone, the mailmen usually left to meet a previously notified date. In the days of sail schooners they were often delayed and so may have had to wait a week or more before returning.

S.H. 293; S.G. 369.

The cargueros, once safely landed and securely lashed were soon driven back to the settlement, though not always without adventures when the occasional load worked loose.

Mostly two men were sent with six cargueros, as lifting and lacing twelve full-woolled skins in bundles was heavy work. The main loads were lashed with a 'manudor'. The method was known as a 'riata' and these days there are probably very few left who could still put on a riata properly. This 'riata' is also known in North America as the 'diamond hitch'. Where the mailman was loading on his own he would hitch up one bight so far, go around to the other side and repeat the operation and so gradually arrive at the same finish of a tightly secured load. The hide used for carguero work and in connection with horse gear generally was from ox hides which had been shaved, stretched at the outside when, trimming off extremities first, a long length was arrived at about one inch to one and a half inches wide according to the thickness of the particular hide. Gradually schooners gave way to steam, and there were many small craft which played their part in earlier days, such as R.M.S. "FALKLAND" and H.M.C.S. "AFTERGLOW", but perhaps the most famous of all was the R.M.S. "FITZROY", another well known Island name, there being a Fitzroy settlement on East Falkland and Fitzroy Street, all named after Captain Robert Fitzroy of the "BEAGLE". Built for the Falkland Islands Co. by Henry Robb Ltd. of Leith, Scotland, and arriving in the Colony as the S.S. "LAFONIA" in November, 1931, she was a 768-ton coaster serving under this name until replaced by the 1,960-ton "LAFONIA" in 1936, when she was given her new name. Under the name "FITZROY" she was used for interinsular service until 1938 when she was put up for sale. However, when the larger "LAFONIA" was requisitioned, she took on, once again, the overseas mail link with Montevideo as well as the inter-island service, a journey of about eleven days, with a few trips to South Georgia and Patagonia.

S.H. 103; S.G. 173.

Apart from being fitted with wireless, she had electric lighting throughout, with wireless telegraph and telephone systems installed. In the inner passageway a list of passengers and their cabin numbers was posted. She carried six double-berth state rooms for first class with dining room, smoke room and lounge. There was also accommodation for eight second class passengers. The "FITZROY", often known as the Falkland Islands postman, was converted to oil burning in 1949, and lengthened to increase her cargo capacity by 20%. She also played a major role in setting up Operation Tabarin.

Communications between Stanley and South Georgia had caused a great deal of concern ever since the commencement of whaling in 1902 and, despite many suggestions and approaches, it was out of the blue that the Falkland Islands Government was informed in April, 1924, that the Tonsberg Whaling Co. had purchased the "FLEURUS" at Boulogne, would be fitting her out for service as a mail ship between Stanley and South Georgia, and were prepared to comply with the terms of the contract making at least one journey annually to the South Shetlands and South Orkneys. For the next nine years she maintained an excellent record for a vessel of 355-tons gross in some of the roughest and most unpredictable seas in the world. She carried the

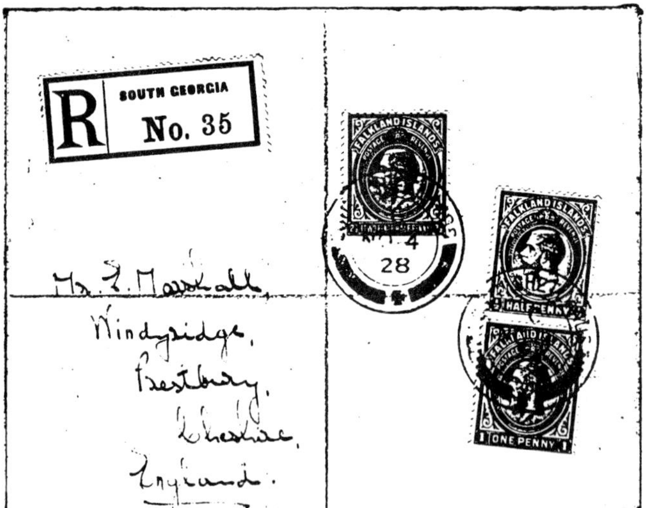

mails from Stanley to Montevideo in 1928 and 1929, served the Islands' community as a coastal steamer carrying passengers, livestock and mail, and on at least one occasion, acted as a hospital ship. The "FLEURUS" was the first regular sea link between Stanley and South Georgia.

S.H. 260; S.G. 336a.

The internal mail from Stanley to the outlying farms and settlements was carried either to Port Howard, Fox Bay or New Island, and was picked up in a variety of ways together with stores and supplies.

The use of steam as against sailing craft in those dangerous waters was an undeniable blessing. The R.M.S. "FALKLAND" took over from the S.S. "COLUMBUS" when it arrived in the Islands in February, 1914. Originally named "WHEATSHEAF" and constructed by Ailan Shipbuilding Co. Ltd. in 1906, she finally left Stanley in January, 1934, after twenty years of constant service, having been sold to a Chilean company in Valparaiso. She weighed only 452-tons, being 52ft. in length.

Lafonia is a name associated with company vessels since the days of their inter-islands schooner at the beginning of this century, one of the few sailing vessels which survived those dangerous waters. The "LAFONIA III" was built at Grangemouth in Scotland in 1911, as the "DOROTHY HOUGH", later changed to "SOUTHERN COAST", and finally to "LAFONIA III" when bought by the Falkland Islands Co. and it is this vessel depicted here. This one deck ship with her Port of Registration as Liverpool, had a net tonnage of 1,228-tons, and underdeck tonnage of 1,438-tons. She was 283ft. long with a breadth of 36ft., and a draft of 18.5ft. Her engines developed 249 N.P.H. The "LAFONIA III" could carry 72 passengers, and went into service in 1937, linking the Islands with Montevideo, a voyage of 1,000 miles which she could achieve in four days. She also carried the mail both inwards and outwards, making occasional calls at Punta Arenas, Brazil, South Georgia and Europe. She provided excellent and reliable service until she was requisitioned for war service in 1941. Unfortunately the following year, whilst sailing in ballast between London and Greenock, she sank in the North Sea following a collision.

S.H. 259; S.G. 335a.

In 1956 it became obvious that a purpose built vessel was required as replacement for "FITZROY". Built at Goole. Yorkshire, the R.M.S. "DARWIN" arrived in August, 1957, and continued her monthly mail, cargo and passenger connections with Montevideo until 1971, with occasional trips to South Georgia, Punta Arenas and Comodoro Rivadavia in the

Argentine. Although an air postal and passenger service was still operating from Montevideo, all still had to commence their journeys by sea from Port Stanley. With a gross tonnage of 1,793-tons, "DARWIN" carried a total of 36 passengers, and had a cargo capacity of approximately 37,000 cubic feet. Mail could be posted on board, of special use to the Islanders when the vessel was travelling around the settlements collecting wool and delivering much needed supplies.

S.H. 256; S.G. 332a.

During these inter-island trips, many of the Islanders used to take advantage of the passenger accommodation --- for Stanley Islanders to visit their friends and relations in the 'camp' settlements, and the 'camp' dwellers to visit town. In every special way, the R.M.S. "DARWIN" provided in a cheap, easy and convenient form, a bond of unity between the remote country dwellers and the 'townies' in Stanley. Her passenger capacity was only fully occupied externally, however, during the seasonal peaks, northbound April to June, and southbound September to November. As far as her deck arrangements and accommodation was concerned, she was known as a flush deck vessel with forecastle and combined bridge and poop. Her machinery was amidships, whilst her accommodation was arranged in both bridge and poop for 16 passengers in 4-berth cabins, and a further 20 passengers in 2-berth cabins. For cargo handling there were three holds with a total capacity of 37,000 cubic feet. However, in later years, it became increasingly obvious to the Falkland Islands Company, particularly during the latter part of the sixties, that she was becoming an increasing financial burden not only to the Colony but also to the Company. Indeed, the Company had drawn heavily on profit from sheep farming to pay the constructional cost of R.M.S. "DARWIN"

With the rapid development of aircraft of all types during World War II, the Governor, Sir Miles Clifford, realising that some major improvements in internal services was essential to the development of the Islands, initiated the purchase of two land-based ex-R.A.F. Taylorcraft Auster 5 aircraft when he was on leave in the U.K. Their letters were once G-AJCH and G-AJCI, c/n 2054 and c/n 817. When they were dismantled they were taken to the Islands by the R.R.S. "JOHN BISCOE", arriving in December, 1948. Subsequently these two aircraft were to be the first to carry a Falkland Islands registration VP-F and were allocated VF-FAA and VP-FAN respectively. When the first was flight tested, that flight was the first in the Falklands by a landplane. Their introduction led to the formation of the Falkland Islands Government Air Service, which greatly reduced the isolation of the settlements. Thus commenced a completely new chapter in internal mail communications, a service which was to progress from strength to strength as the initial problems were gradually overcome. In the opening year of operations F.I.G.A.S. carried a total of 29 passengers, and of these 20 were Government officers on duty and the balance private passengers. In addition drops of mail were made to outlying settlements, the first flight from Stanley to Fox Bay, my old home, taking place on 15 November, 1949. However, the availability of this service was rather more restricted than was at first realised

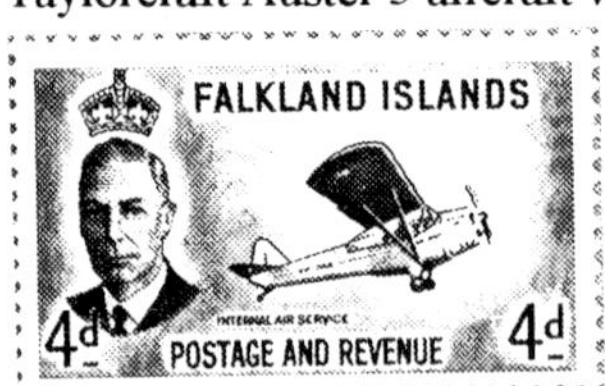

S.H 107: S.G. 177.

as the Austers could only land where settlements had adequate grass air strips and these were very few and far between.

However it had been realised for some time that floatplanes were potentially more useful in the Islands due to the lack of suitable airstrips, and the proximity of all the farming communities and their woolsheds to water. Most, if not all, of the settlements had jetties for inter-island ships, to which floatplanes could be moored to load and unload mail, passengers and a limited amount of freight. It was a small but significant start to an enterprise which had begun primarily as an air ambulance service.

The increased capacity enabled the fledgling air service to develop and passengers began to be carried on a slightly more regular basis. The F.I.G.A.S. order of priorities was, and still is, clearly defined: medical or air ambulance requirements, postal duties, conveyance of passengers and freight. The exact date on which the air service became known as the Falkland Islands Government Air Service (F.I.G.A.S.) has proved impossible to determine, for the acronym started as an idea and was gradually adopted more by usage than by official pronouncement.

S.H. 175; S.G. 246.

Government and F.I.G.A.S. officials involved with the future of the Air Service knew that before too long replacement aircraft would have to be procured. The type selected was the rugged and reliable D.H. Canada Beaver which, when equipped with floats, could fulfil F.I.G.A.S. requirements for the foreseeable future. No more than two Beavers were on charge at any one time, but losses, disposals and their subsequent replacements account for a further five of these sturdy aeroplanes being delivered between 1958 and 1979.

In 1977 a F.I.G.A.S. review committee was formed to consider suitable types of twin-engined landplanes for future operations. However, the possibility of adding a third Beaver floatplane to the inventory was not discounted although there was a general feeling that the Air Service should gradually evolve into a landplane fleet using new and improved old Auster airstrips. In the meantime, the conflict and its immediate aftermath took their toll of F.I.G.A.S. aircraft, equipment and facilities. The two Beavers in use at the time of the occupation were grounded and immobilised by the Argentinians. One was demolished by British bombardment on 11 and 12 June while parked outside the aeroplane hanger, and the other, although assessed as repairable after the war, was blown over onto its back in a gale on 28 July that year and completely wrecked. It was not until January, 1983, that a newly acquired second-hand Beaver floatplane enabled F.I.G.A.S. to recommence operations. This aircraft remained in service until January, 1985, when it was withdrawn and shipped to the U.K. for storage pending sale abroad.

For more than two and a half years a Royal Navy hovercraft saw service in the Islands, and it soon became a familiar part of life. Within a relatively short time they learned the vagaries of sudden increases in wind and sea; where the different species of wildlife were to be found; where the best beaches, kelp-beds and hover-ways were. There was some concern felt by the inhabitants regarding safety, fearing it might break up on the rocks if it ever broke down. Actually it was safer than driving a Landrover across the 'camp'.

Bearing in mind their main task of mobility and support for the Royal Marines in the

The S.R.N. 6 Hovercraft.

defence of the Islands, their job naturally brought them into close contact with the civilian population, and mail was carried at varying times. Although in many places the coastline is extremely forbidding with treacherous rocks and breaking surf, it is nonetheless excellent hovercraft country, with a surprising number of bays and inlets as well as superb beaches.

As for internal communications the decision was finally made to seek the assistance of all settlements in the establishment of suitable landing strips, and to purchase the superb little aircraft, the Britten-Norman Islander, with very short landing and take-off requirements, but which could carry nine passengers, all the mail and a considerable amount of freight. This aircraft is now the general purpose 'workhorse' or 'internal bus service' of the Falkland Islands operated by F.I.G.A.S. This aircraft can be flown as a freighter, with the seats removed, as an executive aircraft or as an ambulance carrying three stretcher cases and two attendants (very effective as I discovered during my stay in the Islands).

S.H. 401; S.G. 463.

THE RAILWAY

During the latter part of World War I, the Admiralty installed a powerful transmitter at Moody Brook, the Royal Marines' base, with such a powerful signal that on one occasion the transmissions were picked up by a sloop of the U.S. Navy on patrol in the North Sea!! Regretfully it came into commission only a few years prior to the invention of the wireless valve which made it obsolete but the costly installation stands as a memorial to the days of the Cape Horn route. The boilers needed large quantities of coal, and for this reason the only railway in the islands was constructed, remaining in service until the later 1920s for naval stores from the naval jetty. The Camber Railway as it was named was a single line 24" gauge approximately 3.5 miles long, built during 1915 and 1916. It ran along the northern bank of the inner harbour from the Camber Depot at Navy Point. Direct radio contact was later established with Norway and England, the contact with Norway being important for those in South Georgia.

S.H. 437; S.G. 500.

S.H. 436; S.G. 499.

About 200 labourers were employed and the first stores included two 'Wren' class locomotives, but what is left of the railway today? There are a few remains and the recovery of one of the engines is being undertaken by the Royal Engineers, together with some sleepers, whilst some tracks have also been found. Unfortunately, at the inshore end of the breakwater was a large dump and over the years more junk was piled on top until the locomotive and rolling stock had virtually disappeared.

OVERSEAS COMMUNICATIONS

With the advent of steam power and the termination once again of the Company contract to carry the mail, a chance arrival of a German Kosmos Line vessel resulted in a mail contract with that Company in 1880, and the "MEMPHIS" was one such vessel. Through co-operation with the Pacific Steam Navigation Co. vessels now worked out a monthly call at Stanley.

Later, the steamers called at Stanley nine times a year in each direction, therefore a three-weekly service.

The 146-ton "MEMPHIS" was the second ship of the Kosmos Shipping Line to make the direct run from Europe arriving at Stanley on 22 September, 1880, and five days out of Montevideo. She was an iron-screw steamer built at Hartlepool, Cleveland, in 1872 by Alexander Withy. Her last call at Stanley was on 10 July, 1897, on her way home from Valparaiso. The Falkland Islands Co. sent their cargos by Kosmos ships, for the mail subsidy alone was not sufficient for steamers to call regularly at the Falklands without the additional revenue from freight. Although the service ran regularly and efficiently for twenty years, the contract was terminated on 1 July, 1900, because the British Post Office was no longer prepared to allow British mail to be carried to and from the Colony on German ships.

S.H. 263; S.G. 339a.

The Pacific Steam Navigation Company, based at Liverpool, had often been a link in the mail chain to Britain collecting the mail bags at Punta Arenas from the Kosmos ships outward bound to the West Coast of South America. Now they entered into a contract with the Government to call at Stanley for the mail and passengers. The arrangements were similar to those with the German company, except that now ships travelling in each direction to and from Valparaiso called at Stanley each month. This meant a collection and delivery of mail fortnightly. The first P.S.N.C. vessel to call was the 5,321-ton "ORAVIA" arriving on 30 July, 1900, one of a fleet which held the Colony's mail contract from 1900 to 1917.

The P.S.N.C. continued this fortnightly service after 1914 when the opening of the Panama Canal caused the main bulk of shipping to avoid the notorious Cape Horn in favour of the shorter route. However, on 18 October, 1912, The "ORAVIA" left Liverpool for the last time. Towards midnight on 12 November, en route for Callao, and making for Stanley in pitch darkness and heavy rain, she ran aground on the infamous Billy Rock, which can be seen just breaking the surface half a mile off Cape Pembroke Lighthouse at the entrance to Port William, the outer harbour. The radio operator managed to contact Stanley and ships immediately came to the rescue. All the crew, passengers, pigs and sheep, together with the luggage and mail were saved. Typical, the Falkland Islanders got out of their beds to look after the 412 passengers and crew as they came ashore and to accommodate them in their houses, the churches and the schools until they could be collected by another ship a week later. Unsuccessful attempts were made to free the "ORAVIA" but when it became obvious she must be abandoned, the master and the remaining crew were taken off by the next afternoon. Fortunately, there was no loss of life.

S.H. 262; S.G. 338a

If mail had to go by sea to Montevideo, it did not matter greatly whether it was on the surface or undersea. On 15 May, 1947, the U.S.A. "SEA ROBIN" (SS 407) commanded by Commander Paul Stimson, left her base at the port of Bilboa in the Panama Canal Zone to

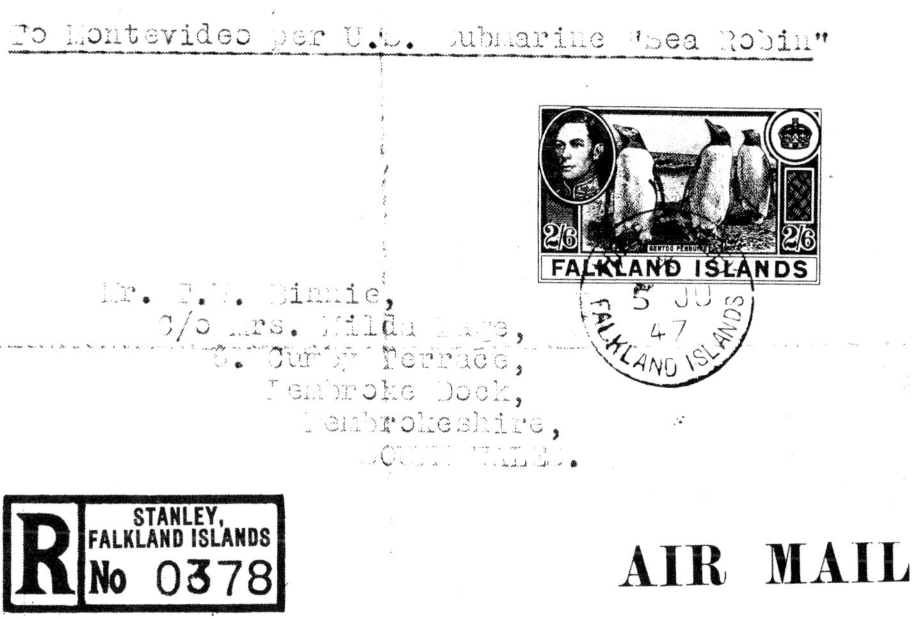

commence a one and a half month simulated war patrol in which she circumnavigated the South American continent, thus becoming the first submarine to round Cape Horn on 1 June. She also became the first American warship to dock at Port Stanley for 50 years, where the weather was cold on that 4 June, but the hospitality warm. Parties of schoolchildren were taken down to the quay to view her before she sailed again on 6 June for Montevideo arriving 10 June. It would appear she carried some mail by favour rather than officially.

April, 1952, saw the first direct air link between the United Kingdom and the Falkland Islands when the Aquila Airways Short S.25 Sunderland III Hythe Class Flying Boat G-AGJN was chartered by the Falkland Islands Company for a survey flight to Port Stanley from Southampton and return. It was the only flight of its kind as it proved very expensive and it

S.H. 270; S.G. 346.

S.H. 271; S.G. 347.

was not envisaged that a permanent service would be introduced, as the charter was really to commemorate the Centenary of the Falkland Islands Company.

The Aquila flying boat at anchor at Stanley.

From 1955 the Falkland Islands Company chartered Danish vessels to bring out the supplies from England and to take home wool from the Islands, and this is represented by the M.V. "A.E.S.", brought into service in 1957. She was under charter throughout the year apart from a few weeks for annual refit, and made four round trips annually from the United Kingdom with stores and from the Colony with wool and sheepskins. Practically all surface mail was also carried on this vessel. These exports from the Colony provided sufficient cargo for only three voyages, so a cargo for a fourth voyage was, therefore, obtained from South America, usually timber from Brazil.

Built in 1957 by Svendborg Skibsaerft, the "A.E.S." was based at Svendborg, and owed her somewhat unusual name to the initials of her owner, A.E.Sorenson. She was also one of the largest vessels in this company's fleet. She first arrived in Stanley on 16 December, 1957, and was finally withdrawn from service when the charter was cancelled because operating costs after seventeen years of such a large vessel became too high. She carried a crew of 21 and had accommodation for twelve passengers. In the Communications Agreement reached with Argentina in 1971, the British Government undertook to arrange a regular shipping service between the Colony and Argentina and in practice this was to be met by a scheme developed by the Falkland Islands Co. involving the diversion of "A.E.S." to Mar del Plata, north and south bound, and round trips to Puerto Deseado from Stanley as necessary.

S.H. 255; S.G. 331a.

WORLD WAR II — THE BATTLE OF THE RIVER PLATE

From the very early days there has been a very strong connection between the Islands and the British Military Forces many of whom carried out early constructional and building work on the Colony. Indeed, on 12 January, 1858, a force of Marines landed to replace the pensioners. In January, 1863, a new detachment arrived to take over from the garrison and Governor D'Arcy completed two new roads with their assistance. The Naval Superintendent relied on the Marines for most of his workmen, and their buildings and corrals often remain to-day. Many of those serving in the Colony obtained their release and remained as colonists, a tradition that has continued until the present time. Little need be said of the Royal Marines' involvement of recent years in the Islands.

S.H. 387; S.G. 448.

The outbreak of the Second World War found the Islands in a good state of preparedness. After Japan entered the conflict in 1941, the Falkland Islands were vulnerable, especially after the Japanese had seized the Marshall Islands, the coaling station for Von Spee's Squadron in the 1914-18 war. There was also a chance that the Japanese could have established a base for refuelling and re-victualling of surface raisers and submarines in Antarctica. Further defence measures were taken, with the maximum age for call-up being raised from 48 to 51. A civil defence unit was set up and blackout was compulsory. Again, Stanley children were evacuated to farm settlements on East and West Falklands with their teachers and

S.G. 670.

some parents. In August, 1942, the 11th West Yorkshires arrived as a garrison force to be succeeded in 1944 by a detachment of the Royal Scots who remained until the end of the war.

Considering its resources and population, the Colony, in both Wars, contributed most generously to the British war effort. In the Second World War, the Government made a donation of £50,000 from which ten Spitfires were bought and flown bearing the name "FALKLAND ISLANDS". The local Red Cross raised over £30,000 for the British Society, and £3,000 for St. Dunstan's. Further contributions were also received for the Beaverbrook Fund, the London Relief Fund, King George's Fund for Sailors and the Flying Bomb Fund, whilst companies and individuals gave interest free loans. Both wars demonstrated one thing clearly. It cannot be said too often, whenever danger has threatened, these small remote and half-forgotten Islands would prove themselves to be not only the most loyal, but the most liberal in the Commonwealth. This design shows men of three Services against the background of the Cross of Sacrifice in Stanley, for their contribution was not only in money but also in lives.

S.G. 599.

S.H. 385; S.G. 446.

At dawn on 13 December, 1939, the lookout on H.M.S. "AJAX" spotted a smear of smoke. H.M.S. "EXETER" investigated and so commenced what has become known as the Battle of the River Plate. On identification of the German surface raider "GRAF SPEE", Commander Harwood divided his little force into two, the "EXETER" acting as one unit, the "ACHILLES" and "AJAX" together as the second. Thus the German ship could be attacked on both sides at once and would be obliged to split her fire. Her self destruction by explosives and scuttling just before sunset a few days later brought a rather ignominious end to the German surface raider which had been causing havoc amongst allied shipping for some time.

H.M.S. "EXETER" was the largest of the attackers with the heaviest armament and the longest range, and so suffered far greater attention. Right at the start great holes were torn in her comparatively thin armour plating, the funnels and searchlights were riddled, her aircraft was badly damaged and the communication system affected. Her first casualties were those killed on the starboard side torpedo tubes. A direct hit later destroyed 'B' -turret and killed all on the bridge except the Captain and two officers, and for a short time she was out of control. A second direct hit started a serious fire, but still the"EXETER" did not give up. She now had a seven degree list and was down by the bows. Despite struggling to continue the battle she finally had to withdraw, limping her way very slowly to the Falkland Islands and the shelter of Stanley Harbour.

There were originally four ships in Commodore Harwood's division, of which H.M.S.N.Z. "ACHILLES" was a 7,000-ton cruiser with eight 6" guns and a maximum range of 25,000 yards, with only 4" steel in vital areas. The "ACHILLES", with the support of H.M.S. "AJAX", opened fire immediately after the "EXETER" at a range of 9.5 sea miles. The

"GRAF SPEE" attacked these two smaller vessels with her 5.9" guns, though one 11" shell, bursting in line with the bridge of the "ACHILLES" about 20 minutes after the start of the battle, caused some damage and killed or wounded several men on the gunnery platform control position and bridge. However, although the captain was wounded in the head and leg, he was able to carry on and keep her in the battle. Equally as much, the raider had had enough, and it was the "ACHILLES" and "AJAX" pursuing her at full speed into Montevideo Harbour. Regretfully their 6" shells were bursting close to or against her heavily armoured side without any obvious effect.

S.H. 232; S.G. 307.

S.H. 233; S.G. 308.

The third of the four vessels which initially made up the Squadron commanded by Commodore Harwood was H.M.S. "AJAX", also his flagship. She, like the "ACHILLES", was a 7,000-ton cruiser armed with 6" guns, and with only 4" steel in vital areas. It was the lookout on the "AJAX" who first sighted the smear of smoke which turned out to be the "GRAF SPEE", and which was to commence the Battle of the River Plate. During the course of the running battle the "AJAX" aircraft had gallantly taken off in the midst of intense gunfire to mark the effect of the ship's gunnery on the enemy raider and likewise reported on the appalling damage sustained by the "EXETER".

By early morning, the cruisers had reduced the range to less than five miles, though at the expense of a direct hit on the afterstructure of H.M.S. "AJAX", which wrecked one gun turret while a shell splinter jammed another. The shell actually exploded in Commodore Harwood's cabin, but he was far from his cabin at the time, and still further from sleep. The British ships began to turn, when it became obvious that the "GRAF SPEE" was running for port, and when turning under a smokescreen, an unlucky shot from an 11" gun brought down the main topmast for the "AJAX", destroying the aerial and causing some casualties. A spare aerial had to be rigged before the Commodore could transmit further signals.

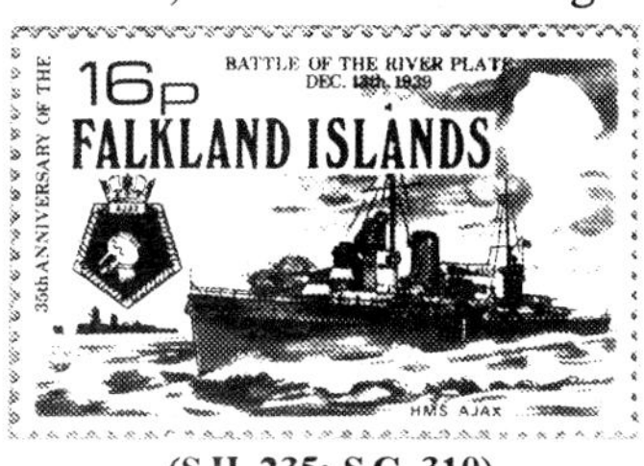

(S.H. 235; S.G. 310)

However, Captain Langsdorff was not only concerned with the condition of his own vessel and crew, but also with the skilfully 'planted' information that several large British warships were already on their way, including the battleship "RENOWN". The fatal decision was that the "GRAF SPEE" was to be scuttled, and on the fifth night of their vigil outside, the "ACHILLES" witnessed the end of their opponent.

The "GRAF SPEE" herself had a total weight of shell in any one broadside of 4,708 lbs, with a range of 30,000 yards. Captain Langsdorff had not at first thought that the British vessels were warships or else he would have turned away. However, despite her superior armament she suffered much damage above the waterline and below, and had an unexploded shell embedded in the hull above the waterline. She had had enough. She had been struck more than 50 times; 37 of her crew were killed and 57 wounded.

S.H. 234; S.G. 309.

All these facts no doubt influenced Captain Langsdorff in seeking shelter in Montevideo, Uruguay. However, according to international law, the vessel must leave almost at once or be interned for the duration. After lengthy negotiations, the "GRAF SPEE" was ordered to leave within the prescribed time or submit to internment. When she steamed slowly seaward every British seaman was convinced the battle was to be renewed. Her self-destruction, when it became known, was greeted with cheers. The Battle of the River Plate was over. The German crew and their officers duly reached Buenos Aires --- only to discover that the Argentinians insisted on interning them. Captain Langsdorff unable to bear the disgrace of losing his ship, spread a flag on the floor and shot himself.

S.H. 533; S.G. 596

THE CONFLICT

Most people believe that the first invasion of the Falkland Islands by the Argentine took place in 1982, but it was in 1966 that an earlier intrusion occurred. On 22 September, a DC-4 airliner landed on the racecourse. The first Islanders on the scene were met by men flourishing guns and were bundled into the aircraft. The next arrivals were handed leaflets intimating that the gunmen had come to take over the Islands on behalf of the country to which they 'rightfully belong', running up the Argentinian flag and demanding to see the Governor. The Aerolineas Argentinas aircraft had been on an internal flight from Buenos Aires to Rio Gallegos in Southern Patagonia when it had been hi-jacked and the pilot forced to divert to the Islands. The 21 hi-jackers belonged to an extreme right wing nationalist organisation called Condor. The idea was that in the year of internal historic significance, 1966 being the 150th anniversary of the Formal Declaration of Independence from Spain of the United Provinces, part of which, in 1853, became Argentina, was to draw attention at the start of another United Nations' session, to the Argentina claim to the Islands.

The siege lasted less than 48 hours, during which the hi-jackers sent out a defiant message of NO SURRENDER to their compatriots in Argentina. As in the subsequent conflict of 1982, they succumbed to the cold and surrendered to the local cleric who had been acting as interpreter. Two days later an Argentine ship arrived in Port Stanley and took away not only the plane's passengers but also the hi-jackers.

The end of the German pocket battleship "Graf Spee".

The crashed hi-jacked aircraft on Stanley race course.

The success of military operations for the recovery of the Falkland Islands must be equally shared amongst the Army, Navy and the Air Force as well as the Mercantile Marine, all of whom played their part in what was truly Combined Operations. The Mercantile Marines were mainly responsible for the transportation of both men and supplies of a Task Force which confounded almost everyone with its speed and organisation. The Royal Navy gave excellent cover and superb support both to the Merchant Navy and the Army when landings were made. The Air Force took on and effectively defeated the Argentine Air Force, despite its most gallant efforts to strike more effectively at the Navy and its transports, whilst it was the Army lads who did the 'yomping' and broke the back of the Argentine Army resistance. The whole affair of liberation was completed by 14 June, but the clearing up took at least a further two years.

S.H. 393; S.G. 454.

Re-heat proved to be virtually useless in combat --- aircraft just cannot dog-fight at twice the speed of sound --- and this was where the slower Harrier came into its own. Its vectored thrust --- which meant the pilot could deflect its jet gases to steer in any direction --- made it as manoeuvrable as a helicopter. So it is a versatile aircraft that can go up, down, sideways, --- even backwards --- pirouetting through the sky like a ballerina. The secret is 'viffing' --- vectoring in forward flight. A Harrier pilot, seeing an enemy aircraft chasing him, pulls a lever in the cockpit and swivels his jet nozzles. Before his pursuer can turn, the Harrier pilot had turned out of his line of fire. Then as the other aircraft overshoots, he fastens on its tail. Suddenly the pursuer becomes the pursued.

S.H. 395; S.G. 456.

As the first ships of the Royal Navy headed south, they were all prepared for action and all unnecessary gear was stowed away or even thrown overboard. Some ships were actually steaming north after a deployment in The Gulf that started before Christmas. They soon had to reverse course. After frantic activity the aircraft carriers "HERMES" and "INVINCIBLE" were ready to leave. Some men were on leave, machinery removed for maintenance and repair, but within a weekend all were in situ and the world's largest warships sailed out of Plymouth.

S.H. 396; S.G. 457.

The restoring of the Falkland Islands to their rightful way of life under the Union Jack was probably one of the greatest naval and maritime expeditions since D-Day in June, 1944. The cruise liner "UGANDA" was taken over on the high seas. She landed her schoolchildren at Naples, and sailed for Gibraltar for a quick conversion to a hospital ship. Other merchant vessels

S.H. 394; S.G. 455.

started arriving at Naval ports for conversion to their new roles. A standard communications link was essential. Cunard's "ATLANTIC CONVEYOR" was brought from Mersey, but this journey was to end in tragedy in the southern waters. Her sister ship, "ATLANTIC CAUSEWAY" had the same conversion. Even Cross Channel ferries were pressed into service as was the BP tanker "BRITISH ESK". Next the "CANBERRA" was taken over and quickly converted as was the North Sea ferry "NORLAND" and finally the "QUEEN ELIZABETH II" herself.

AIR TRAVEL

Under the Communications Agreement of 1971 signed by Great Britain and Argentina, Britain agreed to provide a permanent airfield in the Falkland Islands; the site selected being on Cape Pembroke, near the lighthouse, to the east of Stanley. Meanwhile a temporary airfield made of aluminium strips was laid down by the Argentine Government at Hookers Point nearby, and provided the external communications with the outside world. Construction of the permanent airfield began at the end of 1974 by Johnson Construction Ltd., and was completed in mid-1977.

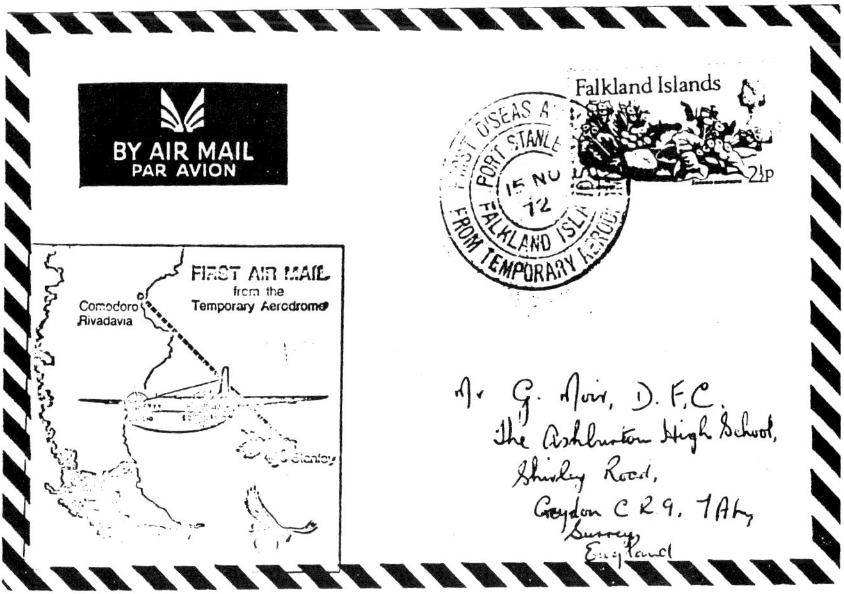

It was put into use at 9a.m. on Thursday, 24 November, 1977, after an unofficial ceremony when a private aircraft both landed and took off, circled and landed again. However, the first mail did not leave the new airfield, now called Stanley Airport, until Thursday, 1 December, 1977, when the Argentine F27 made the first scheduled landing and, later that day, took off carrying the weekly overseas mail including specially postmarked covers. From 17 May, the weekly flight was supplemented by a Fokker VFW F28 Fellowship of LADE, thus doubling the number of overseas flights into and out of the Islands. As far as internal services were concerned, the most popular aircraft and that still in great service, is the Britten-Norman Islander.

By far the most significant result of the Falkland Islands conflict in 1982 was the construction of the magnificent airport at Mount Pleasant, able to accept wide bodied jets of international size, so that direct travel to and from the Islands at last became a reality. There has been no further reliance upon Argentina for this vital communication.

(S.H. 286; S.G. 362.)

RADIO AND TELEPHONE COMMUNICATIONS

The amateur radio operator had his own niche in the communications system of the Falkland Islands. He has played an important part in communication history with amateur radio sets being used when official circuits have failed. In 1979 a change in the Wireless and Telegraphy Regulations permitted part of the 2-metre band to be used for social, commercial and limited business purposes in addition to normal amateur use. This led to a large involvement in amateur VHF equipment and the establishment of an extensive private communications network especially in the 'camp'. The majority of these sets operate only in the 2-metre band.

S.H. 252; S.G. 328.

That does not mean there never was a telephone system in the Islands. In fact, in 1890, the Falkland Islands Company made proposals for linking Stanley with their main farm; but it was not until 1897 that the first line came into operation between Cape Pembroke Lighthouse and Stanley. The Darwin line came into operation in 1907, and the entire system became so popular that a public exchange had to be constructed, which brought about the first broadcasting services. The telephone service to the 'camp' settlements gradually fell into a complete collapse for many reasons and the most important form of internal radio communication, apart from the 2-metre set, became the Government operated radio telephone service. However, in much more recent times (after 1982) a new telephone service has been installed which, with the assistance of Cable and Wireless, has made telephone communication from the U.K. possible even to the remotest farms.

S.H. 253; S.G. 329.

The loss of shipping anywhere is a serious matter, but losses in and around the Falkland Islands prompted the installation of wireless communications with the outside world. External communications in those early days of this century made contacting agents a long drawn out time --- often relying on other shipping to inform them of their fate. Lloyds had long established an agency within the Islands, but the need for some swifter form of communication was called for.

S.H. 254, S.G. 330

A station was established by the Marconi Wireless Telegraph Co. three miles out of Stanley capable of reaching Buenos Aires and Montevideo, and in 1974 the handling of external communications was taken over by Cable and Wireless Ltd. Through this there is now a Telex service and a public telegram service. A direct telephone service between Stanley and Buenos Aires was opened in 1972 as part of the Communications Agreement with that country.

GOVERNMENT HOUSE

Quite close to the Cable and Wireless office is the seat of Government, and during those tragic days of 1982, most of the early fighting took place around Government House. Work on the present building was commenced in 1845 by Governor Moody. Initially the building erected appears to have been used as public offices and not for residential purpose. Governor Moore completed the stone building which contains the drawing room below and the Governor's bedroom and he took up his official residence there in 1859. Between 1881 and 1883, Governor Kerr added the present western wing to accommodate four bedrooms and two attics. This roof is covered with shingles and there still exists, above what is the Governor's office, some iron roofing, since covered over.

(S.H. 382; S.G. 443.)

On that wonderful day in June, 1982, when the Union Jack was hoisted once more on the flagpole in the grounds of Government House, part of the message sent to Her Majesty the Queen read: "The Falkland Islands are once again under the Government desired by their inhabitants." Thankfully, it continues to be so, but there have been decided difficulties to overcome during these post-conflict years. Certainly, thanks to the Shackleton Report, virtually every farm on the Islands now belongs to an Islander, but the price of wool has become disastrously low, to such an extent that many of these young sheepfarmers are finding it difficult to sell their wool clips at viable prices.

FIRE HAZARDS

Fire can be both damaging and dangerous at all times and during the summer season can cause many problems in the 'camp', with fire burning down into the peat and only flaring up when the wind is favourable. Nothing could be more serious than the two major fires which have affected the Colony. The first, in 1944, was the complete destruction of the Town Hall and Post Office. The second, in April, 1984, was the complete destruction, this time involving some fatal casualties, of the old King Edward VII Memorial Hospital. Now, thanks to the most generous contributions from many sources, a new modern hospital, serving both civilian and military personnel has arisen.

S.H. 491; S.G. 554.

ANTARCTIC CONNECTION

Ships and shipping have always been to the fore in almost every aspect of Falkland Islands' life and H.M.S. "ENDURANCE" has been at its heart for many years. There have been several occasions when concern has been felt about the possibility of withdrawal; but, sadly, the time had to come for her final voyage. She had been built in 1956 and most of her commission time had been in these southern waters. There was also anxiety over whether she would be replaced, but the British Government eventually purchased the Norwegian vessel "POLAR CIRCLE", completed in 1990, to continue the presence of the White Ensign in the South Atlantic and for Antarctic ice patrol, and she has been appropriately renamed H.M.S. "ENDURANCE".

THE FUTURE

The future of the Falkland Islands looks promising, providing it is the WISHES of the Islanders which are taken into consideration and not their interests. Their constantly declared wish has been to remain British, and they have demonstrated this and their loyalty to Britain in a number of ways. Young Islanders are either remaining or returning after completing their education in Britain. Thanks to the Fishing Conservation Zone, a far greater income to the Colony in now enjoyed enabling more development to be undertaken than ever before and, thanks to the construction of Mount Pleasant Airport, more and more people are taking the opportunity to see the Falkland Islands for themselves. That the recession in world trade has had an effect on farming in the islands is reflected in the still low prices for wool fleeces on the international market, but this is likely to readjust in the foreseeable future. Seeing is believing and the Falkland Islands need to be better understood, and are well worth maintaining and retaining under the British flag.

I only hope that it will not be too long before I am able to make a return visit to those Islands and to the people with whom I lived and worked for some extremely happy and rewarding years.

FALKLAND ISLANDS DATES

1592 First sighted by John Davis, English navigator in the *Desire*.

1594 Sir Richard Hawkins confirmed Davis' discovery when he sailed along the northern shores of the Islands and identified various geographical features.

1690 First recorded landing by Captain Strong of the *Welfare* in the sound separating the two main islands. Named this Falkland Sound after Viscount Falkland, Treasurer of the Navy.

1764 Antoine Louis de Bougainville established the first settlement on the Islands in Berkeley Sound, East Falkland. Named it Port St. Louis after the French King.

1765 British Naval Squadron under Captain John Byron survey the Islands and hoist Union Jack on Saunders Island, West Falkland. Named Port Egmont after the Earl of Egmont, First Lord of the Admiralty.

1766 British settlement established at Port Egmont under Captain John Mc Bride, who named the whole archipelago Falkland Islands.

1767 Spain objected to French settlement. Bougainville forced to sell. Spanish garrison replaced French settlers. Port Louis renamed Puerto de la Soledad.

1770 Strong Spanish expedition from Buenos Aires compelled surrender of British at Port Egmont. Spain and Britain prepared for war, but this was averted by Spain's disavowal of Buenos Aires expedition.

1771 Port Egmont restored by Spain to Britain.

1774 British garrison withdrawn for reasons of economy. Lead plaque left behind declaring Falkland Islands to be the sole property of George the Third, King of Great Britain.

1811 Spanish Governor of Montevideo withdrew garrison from Puerto de la Soledad.

1811-20 Islands uninhabited except for North American and British sealers who used them as headquarters for sealing activities in the South Atlantic.

1820 Captain Daniel Jewitt, Colonel of Buenos Aires Marine, ran up the flag of the United Provinces at Port Soledad.

1823 First expedition to the Islands initiated by partnership of Louis Vernet and Jorge Pacheco from Buenos Aires under command of Robert Schofield was a failure.

1826 Vernet's second expedition to the Islands.

1828 Buenos Aires Government granted Vernet permission to form a colony and given grant of all East Falkland together with sole rights to seal and fish.

1829 Vernet appointed Governor. Britain protested.

1831 Vernet arrested three North American schooners for illegal sealing: the *Harriet* with herCaptain taken to Buenos Aires for trial. US Consul in Buenos Aires arranged dispatch of corvette *Lexington* to Port Soledad to destroy settlement. Accomplished December and Matthew Brisbane, in charge of the settlement, taken to Montevideo in irons.

1832 Buenos Aires appoints new Governor, but on arrival murdered by mutinous soldiers.

1833 (January) Captain Onslow arrived in HMS *Clio* to retake possession of the Islands. HMS *Tyne* followed. William Dickson, senior British resident, put in charge of the British flag.

1833 (April) Matthew Brisbane returned to re-establish the settlement.

1833 (August) Gauchos led by Antonio Rivero murdered Brisbane, Dickson and others. Surviving settlers took refuge on small island in Berkeley Sound.

1833 (October) Lt. Rea arrived on sealer *Hopeful* and provided temporary relief.

1834 (January) HMS *Challenger* arrived accompanied by *Hopeful*. Lt. Henry Smith, First Officer of *Challenger*, with a boat crew left in charge of settlement.

1834 (March) Rivero and gauchos arrested, taken to Rio and thence to England, but no trial and all returned to Montevideo by Admiralty.
There has been continuous, effective and peaceful possession, occupation and administration by Britain of the Falkland Islands from 1834 until 1982.

1853 Republic of Argentina established.

1881 Falkland Islands ceased to be grant-aided and became financially independent of Britain.

1914 (November) Battle of Coronel.

1914 (December) Battle of the Falkland Islands.

1939 Battle of the River Plate.

1942 Garrison (the West Yorkshire Regiment) placed in the Falkland Islands to defend the Islands from Japanese attack.

1968 Falkland Islands Committee formed to express the wishes of the Islanders.

1976 Major Economic Survey of the Islands conducted by Lord Shackleton.

1982 (April) Argentine illegal invasion of Falkland Islands.

1982 (May) British Task Force land at San Carlos.

1982 (June) Argentine Forces surrender and freedom restored to the Falkland Islands.

BIBLIOGRAPHY

1. "THE FALKLAND ISLANDS" by Ian Strange.
2. "THE FALKLAND STORY" by Mary Cawkell.
3. "CROWN AGENTS
4. THE NATIONAL MARITIME MUSEUM LIBRARY.
5. "DARWIN'S DESOLATE ISLANDS" by Patrick Armstrong.
6. "THE FALKLAND ISLANDS" by M.L.R. Cawkell, D.H. Malling, and E.M. Cawkell
7. "THE IRON SHIP" by Ewan Corlett.
8. LIVERPOOL MARITIME MUSEUM
9. "CHRIST CHURCH CATHEDRAL" by Gervase Murphy.
10. "THE LIFE AND WORK OF BISHOP STERLING".
11. "WHALES AND DOLPHINS" by Dr. Antony R. Martin.
12. FALKLAND ISLANDS' ARCHIVES.
13. THE FALKLAND ISLANDS JOURNAL.
14. "THE POSTAL SERVICE OF THE FALKLAND ISLANDS" by R.F. Barnes.